THE NECESSITY OF SECULARISM

THE NECESSITY OF SECULARISM
Why God Can't Tell Us What to Do

RONALD A. LINDSAY

PITCHSTONE PUBLISHING
Durham, North Carolina

Pitchstone Publishing
Durham, North Carolina
www.pitchstonepublishing.com

Library of Congress Cataloging-in-Publication Data

Lindsay, Ronald A. (Ronald Alan)
   The necessity of secularism : why God can't tell us what to do / Ronald A. Lindsay.
      pages cm
   Summary: "For the first time in human history, a significant percentage of the world's
population no longer believes in God. This is especially true in developed nations, where in
some societies nonbelievers now outnumber believers. Unless religion collapses completely,
or undergoes a remarkable resurgence, countries across the globe must learn to carefully
and effectively manage this societal mix of religious and irreligious. For in a world already
deeply riven by sectarian conflict, this unprecedented demographic shift presents yet another challenge to humanity. Writing in an engaging, accessible style, philosopher and lawyer Ronald A. Lindsay develops a tightly crafted argument for secularism—specifically, that
in a religiously pluralistic society, a robust, thoroughgoing secularism is the only reliable
means of preserving meaningful democracy and rights of conscience. Contrary to certain
political pundits and religious leaders who commonly employ the term secularism as a
scare word, Lindsay uses clear, concrete examples and jargon-free language to demonstrate
that secularism is the only way to ensure equal respect and protection under the law—for
believers and nonbelievers alike. Although critical of some aspects of religion, Lindsay neither presents an antireligious tirade nor seeks to convert anyone to nonbelief, reminding us
that secularism and atheism are not synonymous. Rather, he shows how secularism works
to everyone's benefit and makes the definitive case that the secular model should be feared
by none—and embraced by all"—Provided by publisher.
   ISBN 978-1-939578-12-9 (paperback)
   1. Secularism. 2. Secularism—Political aspects. 3. Religious pluralism—Political
aspects. 4. Freedom of religion. I. Title.
   BL2747.8.L56 2014
   322.1—dc23
                              2014013748

For David and Anne

"This fair child of mine shall sum my count and make my old excuse."
Shakespeare, Sonnet 2. 10–11.

CONTENTS

INTRODUCTION

"The devil caught you at third base." The nun who uttered that admonition to me when I was seven years old—after I had erred in making the sign of the cross (going right before left)—didn't realize how prophetic she was. At least from a Catholic perspective, the devil did catch me when I was about twenty-one, as that is when I ceased to believe in God.

The transition from Catholic to atheist did not take place overnight. It was an emotionally wrenching process that took several months, causing many sleepless nights, a sense of anomie, and anxiety attacks. I was not a nominal Catholic. I believed deeply and I hewed closely to the official Church position on just about everything. The first article I ever had published consisted of a highly polemical essay against contraception. Before I stopped believing, I had even taken preliminary steps to becoming a priest. (That I did not become a priest, thereby undoubtedly sparing the Church much trouble, may be the one authentic miracle the Church can claim.) Giving up my beliefs was not easy.

That said, I have no resentment or regrets over the fact that I was raised Catholic. In fact, in retrospect I regard it as fortunate that I remained a Catholic until early adulthood. Why? It gives me some understanding of the perspective of believers: why they hold fast to their beliefs and how many of them tend to view moral issues. My experience also dispels one myth about the religious accepted by all too many atheists—namely, that the religious are stupid. No, I don't think I was stupid when I was younger, just mistaken.

The fact that I have been both a believer and a nonbeliever also gives me a heightened awareness of the novel, challenging situation in which the United States and many other countries now find themselves. For the first time in human history, we have substantial numbers of nonbelievers living side by side with believers. Moreover, this is a situation that is likely to persist for some time. The number of nonbelievers is going to increase in developed countries, but religion is not going to disappear in a few years, if ever.

One shared problem we face going forward is that believers often do not speak the same language as nonbelievers, especially when it relates to moral issues or public policy questions that have moral dimensions. I know. When I was a believer, my views on moral issues were based principally on scripture or the teachings of the Catholic Church. Even the positions I held that appeared to be derived from secular reasoning frequently had a religious base. Scrape the top off an argument that supposedly relies on natural law and you're likely to find theology underneath.

Taking positions based on religious doctrine may seem to work well enough in a society where one religion dominates. It definitely does not work well in a religiously pluralistic society that includes not only diverse religious groups but also a large number of nonbelievers. If believers persist in relying upon religious doctrines in public policy matters they will fail to engage those who do not speak their religious language. A well-functioning democracy requires citizens to talk to each other in terms everyone can understand. I don't think a breakdown in democratic discourse will necessarily lead to violence, but it may lead to the fracturing of our societies along religious lines, with political parties becoming aligned with different religious (or irreligious) groups. The push for sharia courts in some European countries may be a harbinger of this development. Already in the United Kingdom, sharia councils have been allowed to arbitrate disputes among Muslims. Although in theory the decisions of these councils must not conflict with British law, this is not always the case. More troublingly, in March 2014, British lawyers were provided with guidance on how to draft sharia-compliant wills that would also be recognized under the British legal system. This is a big step toward the creation of a parallel legal system. Creation of parallel legal systems for people of different faiths would not be an auspicious turn of events. Indeed, it would mean the end of the notion that "there is one law for all." We should do everything we can to avoid such an outcome.

We need to foster a truly democratic society, in which all persons are treated alike and all persons have a voice in governance. To achieve that end, at a minimum, we must respect those with different religious views. One important step we can all take is not to judge people based on their religious beliefs (and, in this context, that includes atheism). These beliefs do not necessarily indicate either a person's intelligence or character. I have known both nonbelievers and believers who were obtuse, despicable, greedy, mendacious, and just plain odious. And I have been fortunate to know many more nonbelievers and believers who were intellectually curious, honorable, generous, trustworthy, and just plain delightful. I don't think my experience is unique.

Another important step believers can take is to recognize that even though they may think they're in touch with God, those communications are not accessible to others. Either God isn't speaking to the rest of us or he is saying something different. If we are to live together in peace, if we are to work together to foster a productive society which benefits everyone and respects fundamental human rights, we need to reason together. God can't tell us what to do. We need to figure that out for ourselves.

And that's essentially the message of this book.

A Note on Terminology and the Scope of the Book

In this book, I often use the terms "nonbeliever," "nonreligious," and "atheist" interchangeably. For most purposes, this should be neither objectionable nor confusing. An atheist is someone who does not believe in God; so too a nonbeliever is someone who does not believe in God. And since religious belief in Western countries is typically associated with belief in a deity, to reject belief in God usually implies one is not "religious," as that term is commonly interpreted.

That said, I recognize the terms are not strictly synonymous. In particular, many who reject belief in God would not label themselves as atheists, even when a full description of their beliefs indicates they are atheists. In part, this is due to the negative connotations associated with the label "atheist." In any event, when context requires, I will distinguish between the terms.

This book addresses a set of issues that would be encountered in many democratic countries that are religiously pluralistic and have a significant number of nonbelievers in their population. However, to maintain the length of the text within reasonable limits and to ensure a coherent narrative, my focus will be on the United States. Where it is clear my analysis cannot be generalized, that will be noted.

"God" is capitalized; I sometimes refer to God with masculine pronouns. These are stylistic choices only and should not be read as implying any sort of belief in a deity or her, his, or its sex, if any.

One

AN UNPRECEDENTED MOMENT
IN HUMAN HISTORY

We're living in the midst of a revolution in human attitudes and be-lief. In much of Europe and North America and other areas of the developed world, such as Australia and Japan, large portions of the population are now nonreligious, that is, they reject belief in God and transcendent spiritual entities of any sort. This is an unprecedented moment in the history of humanity. As far as we can tell, belief in gods and spirits was nearly universal until the late eighteenth century; widespread religious skepticism, such as we are now experiencing, is a phenomenon of just the last few decades.

The consequences of this dramatic shift in beliefs are still unknown, because we are living through this change. All we can say with certainty at the present is that we're in unfamiliar territory. Humanity has never been in this situation before.

The steep decline in religious belief is most evident in Europe. Some sociologists have referred to Scandinavian countries as societies "without God."[1] The Czech Republic, the United Kingdom, Germany, France, Belgium, and The Netherlands also have substantial nonreli-gious populations.[2]

Even in the United States, often considered an exception to the secularizing trend of many Western countries, there has been a significant growth in the number of individuals who reject belief in God. The American Religious Identification Survey, conducted in 2008, revealed that roughly 12 percent of Americans do not profess belief in God and another 12 percent reject belief in a personal God.[3] Effectively, for one out of four Americans there is no personal, interventionist deity who plays a significant role in their daily lives. God either isn't there or God is largely irrelevant.

The Pew Research Center's 2012 survey analyzing "nones," that is, individuals who have no religious affiliation, showed a similar trend away from religion, at least organized religion. The Pew study revealed that 20 percent of Americans are not affiliated with any particular religion—an increase of 5 percent in just five years.[4]

Moreover, this trend away from religion may be accelerating because young people tend to be less religious than their parents and grandparents. A recent study looking at college age students in the United States found that about 28 percent declared themselves "secular," with almost all these individuals rejecting belief in a personal God.[5]

To what can we attribute this dramatic change? No one really knows, although theories abound. Some attribute it to higher standards of living, increased longevity, and more secure social safety nets, which remove some of the anxieties that motivate some people to turn to God for help. Others maintain education has played a significant role. People are more acquainted with arguments against the existence of God, and science has explained many things that previously were considered God's work, simply because they couldn't be explained otherwise. A contributing factor may be the "snowball" effect, that is, once public unbelief reaches a certain level, the pace at which religion is abandoned accelerates. If one's friends and colleagues are giving up religious belief, can this atheism thing be that bad?

All these factors, as well as several others, may be at work. Religious belief is a complex phenomenon, with many different causes and many different levels of commitment. Similarly, there is presumably no single, simple explanation for unbelief.

But although the turn away from God is undeniable in many Western countries, it is important to remember that substantial portions of the population remain religious even in the most secular countries. Indeed, in only a few countries do nonbelievers have either a majority or something close to it. With respect to the United States, while about 25 percent of Americans reject belief in a personal God, about 70 percent of Americans are convinced there *is* a personal God.[6] And, of course, in Africa, Asia, and South America, religion still has billions of adherents, some of whom are attracted to the more fundamentalist variants of religious belief.

So how will this revolution play out? Will the twenty-first century represent God's last stand, with belief in monotheism waning rapidly so that God will go the way of the gods, and most people will no longer believe in God any more than they believe in Zeus? Will nonbelief plateau at a certain point, with much of the population remaining religious? Or are we at the high water mark for disbelief, with a rollback coming? A religious rebound could be fueled by a resurgent Christianity in Russia, China, and South America and a militant Islam in many parts of the world—including Europe, where Islam has gained a foothold even as much of the population spurns its traditional Christianity.[7]

The rise and fall of religious beliefs is difficult to predict with assurance. It's doubtful whether many Romans in the early second century would have predicted the rise of Christianity, whether many Europeans in the early sixteenth century would have predicted the Reformation and the subsequent rejection of Catholicism by much of the continent, whether many Americans in the early twentieth century would have foreseen the simultaneous decline of mainstream Protestant denominations and the rise of Protestant fundamentalism, or whether many in the West anticipated the recent spike in atheists, agnostics, and other nonbelievers. Perhaps over the next one hundred years some faith will sweep aside other beliefs; perhaps religious beliefs in general will decline precipitously and all but disappear. Either outcome is possible.

However, a much more likely outcome is a significant increase in the number of nonbelievers, accompanied by a decrease, but not a collapse, in the number of believers. This increase could come fairly quickly if nonbelievers reach a critical mass, which would allow for greater acceptance and the sense among many nominal believers that it's no longer socially injurious to acknowledge that one is an atheist or agnostic. The big break in the United States will come if and when a number of politicians who are open atheists are elected to public office. At that point look for many silent atheists and nominal believers to come out of the closet. But even if there is an exponential increase in the number of nonbelievers, it's improbable that religion will be completely abandoned. Religious belief is resilient. Some debate whether religious belief has a genetic basis, but regardless of whether it has a biological foundation, it's undeniable it has deep cultural and psychological roots. Beliefs that have had a firm grip on the human psyche for millennia are unlikely to vanish in a century.

In other words, at least in the developed world, we are likely to have a situation where for several generations we will have a "mixed" population, with those who see no need for religion living alongside those for whom religion still plays an important role in their lives. This has never happened before.

This mix of religious beliefs could pose a danger to social harmony. History bears witness to the fact that differences in religious belief have caused conflict, sometimes violent conflict. Certainly, some Christians, from former Pope Benedict XVI to evangelical Protestants to conservative American politicians and journalists, have expressed concerns about the implications of waning belief in God. In pushing back against the tide of disbelief, they have generally not pointed to what they consider atheism's intellectual deficiencies. No, instead they have vigorously argued for two propositions: one, that in many Western countries religious individuals are now the victims of discrimination and are being persecuted, and, two, that religion is necessary for morality and without a secure religious foundation, a society will degenerate.

Interestingly, the word used by many religious individuals to sum up their fears is "secularism." Pope Benedict warned repeatedly of secularism, usually prefacing it with adjectives such as "radical" or "aggressive."[8] In the United States, those on the Religious Right employ "secularism" as their favorite punching bag, while conservative politicians try to rally their supporters by portraying secularism as an imminent, dire threat. For example, Newt Gingrich, considered by some to be a conservative intellectual, breathlessly entitled his 2010 bestseller *To Save America: Stopping Obama's Secular-Socialist Machine.*[9]

For some, secularism has become the ultimate scare word. Those who use it as a means to frighten and motivate their supporters typically don't provide a clear definition of what they mean by the term, but it obviously is intended to connote something evil and oppressive. Secularism is an insidious menace; it will get you if you don't watch out. If secularism triumphs, it will be illegal to pray, religious people will be herded into camps, and white bread will be outlawed.

What's interesting and ironic about this hysteria over secularism is that secularism, properly understood, is the best protection religious believers have, particularly in a society they no longer control. Secularism protects freedom of conscience, including freedom of religion; it doesn't threaten it.

One reason some may have such dread of secularism is that they mistakenly equate secularism with atheism (and they further equate atheism with suppression of religion). But secularism and atheism are distinct views and don't even belong in the same category; secularism is a political/ethical philosophy; atheism is a belief about the ultimate nature of reality, that is, it's the belief that there is no deity. Espousing one of these views does not entail acceptance of the other.

What is secularism and to what is one committed when one embraces it? I will discuss the secular state and secularism in the next two chapters, but for now secularism should be understood as the view that: government should not involve itself with religious matters; religious doctrine should play no role in shaping public policy or in the discourse about public policy; and religious institutions and beliefs should not enjoy a privileged position within society.

This stance on the role of religion in public life does limit the role of religion, especially religious institutions, in public affairs. However, it is perfectly compatible with respect for freedom of conscience and the absolute right of an individual to come to her or his own conclusions about religious issues. It only requires all citizens, religious and irreligious, to respect others by not seeking to impose views derived from dogma or doctrine. Moreover, in a religiously pluralistic society, secularism is the only reliable means of preserving public order and freedom for all. The alternative is either a particular religion trying to secure a dominant position or religious institutions in general trying to secure a dominant position. Neither alternative is defensible in principle or feasible in a society that is religiously pluralistic, especially one that has a mix of believers and nonbelievers.

Some of the religious may balk at the position that religious doctrine should play no role in shaping public policy because some of our policies are informed by our moral judgments. These individuals may well ask, "If religion is the basis for morality, how are we to ground our policies if we do not allow religious values to influence our public policy?" The appropriate response to that question involves denying the assumption that underlies the question, in other words, denying the proposition that religion is the basis for morality. Of course, denying this proposition is not the same as establishing that the proposition is false, and I'm sure many religious people will think I cannot possibly show that morality is independent of religion.

The belief in the supposed necessary connection between religion and morality remains widespread, being shared by many preachers, politicians, and pundits, as well as billions of believers. This belief accounts for much of the distrust with which nonbelievers are still regarded. After all, if someone doesn't believe in God, and the prospect of reward or punishment for one's actions, how can we expect that person to act morally? Even those who grudgingly concede that the individual atheist may be a decent person regard this as a fortuitous event. So-and-so is a good person *despite* their atheism. As political columnist Michael Gerson has written, "Atheists can be good people; they just have no objective way to judge the conduct of those who are not."[10]

Historically, there has been a relationship between religion and morality. That cannot be denied. However, this is *not* the result of any logical connection between religion and morality, but rather a result of the ways in which most cultures have sought to inculcate and reinforce moral values. Religion is the vehicle through which we have traditionally expressed our moral values, so it's perhaps understandable that many people equate the medium with the message. Nonetheless, moral values didn't originate in religion, nor are they ultimately based on religious doctrines. The fact is that there are certain moral values, principles, and rules (which I will refer to collectively as moral norms) that have been accepted by most people across different cultures regardless of their religious beliefs. This core morality, or common morality, can provide the foundation for discourse about public policy that does not incorporate religious doctrines. We need to focus on our shared values—of which there are many—as opposed to whatever source of inspiration we may find for adhering to these values.

Morality, and its connection to religion, will be the subject of the middle chapters of this book. These chapters are critical for the defense of my central thesis. As indicated, if I am to make a persuasive case for keeping religion entirely out of public policy debates, including public policy debates that have moral dimensions, I need to show that morality has a secular basis, and that believers and nonbelievers can talk to each other about issues of common concern without reference to divine directives.

In chapters 4 through 6, I show that morality is based on human needs and interests. We are all familiar with these needs and interests, and we can consider and discuss how best to address these needs and further these interests using reason and evidence. We can resolve our differences, or at least limit the extent of our disagreements, without bringing God into the picture.

Moreover, it's a good thing that we can resolve our moral disagreements ourselves because we can't rely on God to tell us what's right or wrong. It's not only that we do not need God to tell us what to do, God *can't* tell us what to do. For those who protest that God instructs us through revelation: how do we know this is God speaking? There have been hundreds, if not thousands, of religions in human history. Which revelation was the authentic one? Which sacred scripture actually reflected the thoughts of God, as opposed to merely the thoughts of its human authors? The Tanakh, the New Testament, the Qur'an, the Book of Mormon? The reality is that a particular revelation is accepted as authentic because, based on our own standards of what's right and wrong, we accept it as God's word. First comes our moral judgment, *then* our judgment that some text represents the word of God.

Some may hesitate to acknowledge the reality that morality is a human institution because this raises the specter of "subjectivity." As Michael Gerson and countless others have asked, if we can't rely on God to instruct us, how can we tell whether anything is wrong? Doesn't it all become a matter of opinion? We need to finally rid ourselves of this specter of subjectivity, which has haunted many a discussion of morality. The objective/subjective distinction as it is commonly deployed obscures more than it illuminates. If we continue to think of morality as something based on rules "from above," then removing the "above" does present us with a problem. But morality should be regarded as a human-centered institution serving human needs. Morality is, and should be understood as, a practical enterprise. Morality serves certain functions, such as providing security to members of the community, creating stability, ameliorating harmful conditions, fostering trust, and facilitating cooperation in achieving shared or complementary goals, and because the conditions under which humans have lived haven't changed that much in fundamental respects, many of our moral beliefs and judgments have stayed the same. All human communities have had rules against lying, stealing, and killing because we could not live together otherwise. The "objective" foundations for morality are found in the underlying circumstances of the human condition.

In the last part of this book, I will discuss why the realization that we cannot rely on directives from God is to be welcomed, not lamented. To begin, we should recognize that if there were a God, he would not want to tell us what to do. As I am an atheist, some may think it presumptuous and arrogant to make this claim, leaving aside the fact that it's wrong. But hear me out.

The metaphor often used to express God's relationship to humans is that of a parent (in the past, invariably a father). Parents want the best for their children, but, they also want their children to become adults, that is, to assume responsibility for themselves. Part of that responsibility entails making decisions about the appropriate course of action without parental instructions.

Consistent with the metaphor of God as parent, we are often referred to by religious traditions as brothers and sisters. If I respect my siblings, I don't try to impose my will on them regarding some possible action that may be relevant to all of us. Instead, I invite them to discuss possible options, and together we reason our way to the best solution. If we are all God's children, we have to take responsibility for reasoning together about how we can best achieve our shared goals while maintaining respect for the dignity and worth of all humans. This is the way a loving God would want us to live our lives—if there were a God.

The believer, naturally, affirms there is a God; we atheists assert there isn't. This is a stark contrast in beliefs. For the responsible theist and atheist, however, this metaphysical question should not affect how they come to grips with issues of morality and public policy. It cannot be allowed to affect how they come to grips with issues of morality and public policy, if theists and atheists are to live together. The only way forward is to reason together.

As one can infer by this point, this is not a book that will present detailed arguments against the existence of God. We are not wanting for such books now, and there is no need for me to duplicate the arguments others have made. There will be some discussion of the strong reasons to be skeptical of the claims of any particular religion, but the focus of this book is not on atheism as a claim about the nature of things; rather, I'm more concerned about the problems presented by a society in which a substantial number of theists coexist with a substantial number of atheists.

I believe it's possible to have a flourishing society even with a deep division between its members about the ultimate nature of reality, but only if we refrain from regarding the person who holds different metaphysical views, in particular different views about the existence or nature of God, as an enemy who is to be converted or contained. In and of themselves, another person's beliefs about God reveal little about the character of that person. Much less do they have any effect on or relevance to others. As Thomas Jefferson famously observed, "It does me no injury for my neighbor to say there are 20 gods or no gods. It neither picks my pocket nor breaks my leg."[11]

Jefferson had it exactly right. The beliefs that others have about God or gods don't hurt me, nor should they prevent me from working with and trusting others. Of course, the conduct of others might hurt me, and if people insist on using their religious doctrines as a basis for public policy and interaction with others, harm can, and probably will, result. As already indicated, in this book I will not argue against the existence of God, nor will I ridicule theistic beliefs. However, I will unsparingly criticize the view that religious doctrines should be allowed to dictate public policy. We can't possibly shape a coherent public policy based on shared norms if substantial segments of the population insist that divine communications are the only basis for morality, whether those communications come from a burning bush, some self-designated prophet, or a rock in a hat. Secularism and a secular, common morality provide the only sound, rational basis for public policy.

There is one last issue to address. Some religious individuals are concerned about the growth of atheism not so much because they fear gross immortalities being committed by atheists, but because they imagine atheism will have some subtle corrosive effect on society. Atheists are portrayed as cold, unfeeling individuals, alienated from life and drifting through it without a sense of purpose. In other words, atheists are nihilists for whom life has no meaning or value. This bogeyman is often paraded around when the devout want to warn of the dangers of atheism.

This claim has no logical or empirical support, as we'll see when it's dissected. It's a myth that should be confined to the trash heap of intellectual rubbish along with many of the other myths about nonbelievers.

Just because I don't get my morals from your God, doesn't imply I have no morals; similarly, just because I don't find significance in being part of a deity's plan, doesn't imply that I find life meaningless. We need to move past absurd stereotypes.

But can we? When I mentioned to a friend the topic of this book, he remarked that, "The problem is, the people who should read the book are the ones least likely to do so." If this proves to be true, then my consolation is that my book's fate is not unique. It will share this characteristic with many other works.

My friend was suggesting, of course, that those who dogmatically insist there is a God who has issued unambiguous directives that we are required to follow are not going to be persuaded by the arguments in this book. A glance at the title may be sufficient to dissuade them from even opening its pages. Perhaps. But I remain cautiously optimistic that exposure to new ideas can *sometimes* influence even the most doctrinaire. Moreover, I am also encouraged by the fact that there currently are millions of religious believers who are convinced of the virtues of secularism and of the futility of trying to base public policy on religious doctrines. Secularism can unite believer and nonbeliever: to some extent it already has.

In any event, this book addresses questions that concern millions of individuals, both religious and nonreligious, and not all of them believe they have ready-made answers to these questions. I invite them to consider the basis on which we can live and work together, acknowledging our differences, but not allowing those differences to be obstacles to achieving the common good.

Two

THE BIRTH OF THE SECULAR STATE

A common reaction to secularism is that it is necessarily antireligious. This reaction is unwarranted. Indeed, as we will see in this chapter, the secular state—obviously, a key component of secularism—was the creation of religious individuals.

Blood gave birth to the secular state: the blood of people who were killed in disputes over religious beliefs. Europe in the sixteenth and seventeenth centuries experienced frequent wars among states and civil wars within states, and the principal cause of these horrific conflicts was differences in religious belief, between Catholics and Protestants and between Protestants of different denominations. Even when a state was nominally at peace, religiously inspired violence did not end, as states would brutally suppress religious dissenters within their borders. Protestants were tortured and executed in Spain and other Catholic countries; Catholics suffered similar treatment in England.

This violence was not condemned by religious officials. To the contrary, Catholic priests applauded the killing of heretics (that is, Protestants) while Protestant clergy endorsed the killing of agents of the anti-Christ (that is, Catholics). After about 13,000 French Protestants were slaughtered in Paris and other cities during the notorious St. Bartholomew's Day massacre of August 1572, Pope Gregory

XIII ordered a special celebratory mass and had a medal struck to com-memorate the event.[1]

For most of us living in the contemporary developed world, the reasons for these bitter disputes seem absurd. One of the main points of contention between Protestants and Catholics was their disagreement over the significance of the Eucharist, the Christian ceremony com-memorating the Last Supper. Catholics insisted that Jesus is really pres-ent in sacramental bread after it is consecrated during mass (the bread literally becomes the flesh of Christ), whereas Protestants scoffed at this belief. As one historian has noted, "At this distance in time it may seem strange that so many of the furies set loose by the Reformation had to do with a wafer of sacramental bread." [2] Nonetheless, this strictly theo-logical dispute caused rage, hatred, executions, and war.

Moreover, the accepted understanding of the role of govern-ment at that time provided theoretical justification for this violence. Government authority depended on the will of God.[3] Recall that mon-archs ruled over almost all European states, and their legitimacy derived from the grace of God. Part of the mission of government was to ensure that the actions of its citizens conformed to God's law, as interpreted by religious authorities. It was the state's obligation to promote actively the spiritual health of each of its citizens, and this entailed protecting them from erroneous religious beliefs that could endanger their im-mortal souls. Heretics were killed to protect true believers from eternal harm. As Thomas Aquinas explained, "it is a much graver matter to corrupt the faith, which quickens the soul than to forge money, which supports temporal life." Accordingly, church authorities had an obliga-tion to excommunicate the heretic and deliver him to the government to be executed in order to protect "the salvation of others."[4]

A transformation in the understanding of the state's role began to take place in the mid-seventeenth century, prompted in substantial part by reflections on the destruction and instability caused by religious conflict. By this time it had become clear that religious differences among Europeans could not be resolved through force. Europe would remain divided between Protestant and Catholic. Moreover, within several European countries, including England, there were religious minorities that stubbornly refused to go away. These could not be extirpated, at least not without some extraordinarily sanguinary efforts. But how could a ruler refuse to fulfill the obligation to promote spiritual health? The answer was to remove religious matters from the scope of government authority, but to support this conclusion, a competing model of the state was needed.

Locke's Arguments for Toleration

John Locke provided that competing model. Locke is the political philosopher usually given the most credit for changing the prevailing understanding of the state's role, due in part to his unquestionable influence on the worldview of subsequent thinkers, including the men who became the founders of the United States. Locke maintained, in his *Two Treatises of Government*, that all humans are by nature free and equal.[5] Governments are instituted by the consent of the people. In other words, humans are not obliged to recognize the authority of a monarch who claims to rule by the grace of God. Political authority, whether placed in a monarch or a collective body like a legislature, derives from the people's consent. Essentially, government is a product of a social contract among the people.

And what powers regarding the enforcement of religious doctrine should a government have on Locke's social contract model? Locke answered this question most directly in *A Letter Concerning Toleration*, perhaps the single most important work on the relations between church and state ever written.[6] Locke argued that the people have instituted government to protect their life, liberty, and property, or their "civil interests."[7] Government authority is limited to protecting "things belonging to this Life"; it does not extend to "the salvation of souls."[8] Therefore, the government has no right to compel people to accept any religious doctrines, "including articles of faith, or form of worship, by the force of [its] laws."[9]

Put simply, religious beliefs are of no concern of the government, and the government should make no effort to force people to accept or act in accordance with religious beliefs.

Locke's primary motivation for limiting the role of government in religious matters was his awareness of and distress over the bloodshed caused by religious strife. But he did not put forward the thesis that government should stay out of religious affairs merely because he thought acceptance of this view would produce more peace and stability. He offered three principled arguments for his thesis, which, properly qualified and stripped of some of Locke's religious rhetoric, are still persuasive, although, as we will see, they are not immune from counterarguments.[10]

Locke argued that rational individuals would not give to the government the power to force everyone to accept the religious doctrines endorsed by the government, because this would mean the state would be given authority to enforce religious doctrines *they* might reject. The government cannot be trusted to make the correct theological judgment. Notice that this argument does not devalue the significance of religious belief. To the contrary, it is precisely because religious beliefs are so important to many individuals that they would not want the government to have control over them.

Locke also argued that granting the government the power to regulate religious affairs would prove futile anyway, if the point of giving government this authority is to enable it to help its citizens obtain salvation. Threats of punishment do not cause a person to give up her beliefs. Threats of punishment could force religious dissenters to feign belief, but an insincere expression of belief is not a ticket to paradise. God does not reward hypocrisy. As Locke put it, "true and saving religion consists in the inward persuasion of the mind, without which nothing can be acceptable to God."[11]

Finally, Locke made use of the wide variety of religious beliefs that people have. (Of course, there is even more variety today than in Locke's time.) If the state imposes the belief favored by its king or legislature, there is no guarantee that it is imposing the correct belief. Again, Locke emphasized that the government is not competent to make judgments on theological matters. If the state controls beliefs, whether a person will be saved or not will depend on where that person is born, an outcome that does not seem designed to maximize the salvation of souls. It is better to allow people to arrive at their beliefs through their own reasoning and discussion with others, as this increases the likelihood that they will be correct in their conclusions.

Locke was a Christian and his arguments reflected the temper of his times: expressions of piety and references to the importance of salvation abound. But if one removes these elements, his arguments for toleration and keeping the state out of religious affairs could be made just as easily today. His key insight is recognizing that governments have no theological competence; they need to concern themselves with this-worldly matters.

In assessing Locke's arguments for toleration, it is also important to note the connections between these arguments and his social contract theory, including his claim that there are certain natural rights. The strength of his arguments for toleration depend, to a large extent, on acceptance of both his contention that the natural state for humans is one of freedom and equality and his contention that the consent of the governed is the only legitimate way in which governments can acquire power. If one rejects these contentions, the first two arguments for toleration lose much of their force. For example, someone committed to the view that a government's legitimacy is based on the grace of God may dismiss the importance of the consent of the governed. Who cares what the people want? It is what God wants that counts. Moreover, Locke's second argument implicitly relies on his claim that individuals have a right to freedom of conscience. It is true that coercion of an individual cannot compel genuine belief by that individual. However, one must remember that the justification offered for religious persecutions was not so much that they helped to save the individual heretic—the person with erroneous beliefs—but rather that they helped those who might otherwise be contaminated with false religious beliefs. Thus, a thoroughgoing theocrat would be unmoved by Locke's arguments for toleration. The salvation of the many takes precedence over any purported right of the individual.

Indeed, some European countries persisted with persecution throughout the eighteenth century. The Spanish Inquisition continued until it was abolished by Napoleon in 1808. Vigorous suppression of any dissenting views kept Spain overwhelmingly Catholic. It also kept Spain backward and impoverished, but some undoubtedly regarded this as the price of preserving the true faith.

I note the limits of Locke's arguments not to make a dry academic point or a purely historical observation. Religious persecution is very much a live issue today, as demonstrated by events in Iran and various countries in the Middle East and Africa. Religious persecution can be found wherever faith-based outlooks give priority to adherence to the dogmas of a particular faith over considerations of freedom of conscience. The fault line between tolerance and persecution lies between those who accept the notion that there are fundamental human rights and those who insist that adherence to God's law trumps anything else. Diplomacy and pressure from the international community can sometimes stop particular incidents of persecution, but eliminating the mind-set that favors persecution requires persuading the persecutors to embrace human rights and to acknowledge that government legitimacy derives from the consent of the governed, not a mandate from heaven.

It is no accident that the first secular state (the United States) was founded at the same time that notions of human rights and popular sovereignty were gaining acceptance. It is also no accident that the United States is a constitutional democracy with a government that has express limitations on its powers. Keeping the state out of religious affairs makes eminent good sense *provided* that one not only recognizes that the state's authority depends on the consent of the governed, but also acknowledges the value of freedom of conscience. These connections between secularism, democracy, and human rights are very important (as I will note throughout this book). The recognition that religious belief and expression belong in a private domain, with which the government cannot interfere, both reflects a secular understanding of government's role and reinforces the secular structure of government.

Before we leave Locke, we need to note that Locke's plea for toleration did not extend to everyone. It did not extend to Catholics or Muslims as they were considered loyal to a foreign power and, therefore, the state had a secular reason for persecuting them. Most notably, especially for our purposes, Locke also maintained that atheists should not be tolerated because they could not be trusted. "Promises, covenants and oaths . . . can have no hold upon an atheist."[12] Here Locke is reflecting the view that morality is based on religion and, in particular, the view that without belief in a God who rewards and punishes, a person will not be motivated to keep promises or tell the truth. This prejudice was nearly universal in Locke's time; it still shapes the views of many today. It's an entirely unwarranted belief, and I'll explain why in chapter 6.

The First Secular State

Locke had a significant influence on subsequent thinkers, including those individuals who provided the political and legal framework for the new nation of the United States. "All the important figures of the founding generation, including John Otis, John and Samuel Adams, James Madison, Thomas Jefferson, Patrick Henry, and Benjamin Franklin, were disciples of Locke."[13] Like Locke, these individuals were all too familiar with the conflicts and strife caused when government interfered with religious beliefs. Not only were they aware of European history, but they were aware of the history of colonial America. Many of the colonists settled in the United States to escape religious persecution. Unfortunately, all too often once they were able to set up their own governments they became as intolerant as the governments from which they had fled. For example, the Puritans who landed at Massachusetts Bay in 1630 consciously set out to establish a theocracy, in which the civil authorities had the power to enforce religious doctrines. The result was persecution of people with disfavored religious views. Quakers were banned from the colony, and those who didn't adhere to this ban were hanged. Other religious dissidents were expelled, such as Roger Williams.[14]

The Founders did not want religious strife to tear apart the new nation. Their concern was appropriate not only given the turbulent history of many colonies, but also in light of the significant religious diversity of the United States at the time of its formation. Given that the United States was overwhelmingly Protestant, "diversity" may seem like a strange word, but the fact is that disagreements among Protestant sects were at the time very significant in the eyes of many believers. Episcopalians, Baptists, Congregationalists, Lutherans, Presbyterians, and Quakers did not always get along.

Furthermore, many of the Founders were firm believers both in natural rights and in the notion that governments had limited authority, namely, the authority delegated to them by the people. This did not include the authority to promote the spiritual health of citizens by prescribing religious doctrines. The Declaration of Independence provides solid evidence of the extent to which Locke influenced the Founders. The Declaration maintains that humans have certain "inalienable rights," including the rights to life and liberty, and that governments were instituted to secure these rights. Governments were not ordained by the grace of God, but rather derived "their just powers from the consent of the governed."

These philosophical views were reflected in the foundational document of the new nation, namely, the Constitution. In particular, the Constitution is drafted in such a way that it makes plain to all that the business of the government is restricted to the promotion and protection of what Locke called "civil interests." Article I, sec. 8 of the Constitution enumerates the powers of Congress. Nowhere in that list is any reference made to the authority of Congress over religious beliefs or doctrines. Religion is not a concern of the government. Furthermore, as indicated by the Preamble, "We the People" have established the government. The government derives no authority from a deity.

Indeed, reference to a deity or particular religious beliefs is not to be found anywhere in the body of the Constitution. What scant reference there is to religion in the Constitution underscores the complete separation of religious matters from government affairs. Article VI of the Constitution discusses religion, but only to make clear that the Constitution expressly prohibits any religious test for public office: "no religious test shall ever be required as a qualification to any office or public trust under the United States."

The Founders succeeded in creating a secular state, that is, a state that concerns itself exclusively with affairs of this world and does not venture into religious matters. The domains of religion and government were kept separate and distinct.

One of the most ridiculous claims that has gained currency among some Religious Right advocates is that the Constitution doesn't provide for separation of church and state because the phrase "separation of church and state" is not itself in the Constitution. What these persons fail to understand is that it would have been redundant to include such a phrase in the Constitution. The document as a whole embodies the view that the government is not to meddle in religious matters. The federal government is given very specific, limited powers only over various secular matters. It has *no* powers relating to religion. The government is secular both in its origin (the consent of the governed) and its function. The government and religious institutions are completely separate and have nothing to do with each other. To insist that the Constitution doesn't mandate separation of church and state because it doesn't contain that phrase is more preposterous than a person who is *not* named as a beneficiary in a will insisting he has a claim on the estate because the will does not specifically exclude him by name.

You will note that so far I have not even mentioned the First Amendment to the Constitution, with its prohibition of any law respecting an "establishment of religion." Despite the significance the First Amendment has justly acquired as a guarantor of religious liberty and of the secular state, one can make an argument that it was unnecessary *provided* the people and the politicians could be relied upon to understand the secular structure of the Constitution. James Madison thought so. Although this is not widely known, James Madison, the person who became the principal architect and chief sponsor of the Bill of Rights, initially opposed any amendments to the Constitution on the grounds that they were unnecessary and confusing. Madison was concerned that adding a declaration of rights would imply the federal government had broad powers and only those rights specified in the amendments were protected. The reverse was true. The government was limited in its powers and the people possessed fundamental rights that could not be abridged or annulled by the government. During the June 1788 ratification debate in the Virginia Constitutional Convention, when concern was expressed that the government might insert itself into religious disputes, Madison argued that under the Constitution, "there is not a shadow of a right in the general government to intermeddle with religion."[15]

But the people wanted reassurance. Although Virginia ratified the Constitution, by a narrow vote of 89 to 79, it also recommended, along with several other states, that Congress draft amendments to the Constitution that would expressly protect "essential and unalienable rights of the people."[16]

Following the Virginia ratifying convention, Madison remained ambivalent for some time about the wisdom of amendments that would expressly insulate certain fundamental rights from government interference, but he eventually decided to throw his support behind such amendments. Perhaps the decisive factor in his decision to unqualifiedly support a bill of rights was a March 15, 1789 letter from Jefferson in which Jefferson argued, among other things, that a declaration of rights would empower the judiciary to act as a check on the government.[17] It is one thing to have a constitution that by clear implication recognizes certain fundamental rights; it is another thing to have a constitution that expressly safeguards certain fundamental rights, thus providing the judiciary with an undisputed legal basis for acting against abuses of power. In any event, when the First Congress convened, Madison became the House of Representatives floor leader for the twelve proposed amendments that eventually became the Bill of Rights.

For my purposes here it is only necessary to show that the First Amendment in no way altered the secular character of the American state. To the contrary, it reinforced it. Certainly, the plain language of the religion clauses of the First Amendment so indicates: "Congress shall make no law respecting an establishment of religion, or prohibiting the free exercise thereof." In other words, Congress is not supposed to do anything that supports or promotes religion, nor is it to interfere with how believers express their beliefs.

The principal argument that has been advanced for the view that the First Amendment permits the government to deviate from its secular character and involve itself in religious matters, at least to the extent of supporting religion in general, is the so-called nonpreferentialist interpretation of the Establishment Clause of the First Amendment. Pursuant to this interpretation, the government can support religion, even financially, as long as the government does not favor or prefer one religious denomination over others.

Although this interpretation of the Establishment Clause has had its adherents, including some justices on the Supreme Court, the non-preferentialist reading of the Establishment Clause has been rejected repeatedly by a majority of the Supreme Court, and with good reason. In interpreting the Constitution, as is true in interpreting any legal document, we should, of course, focus on the final language of the document, but the evolution of that language can also be instructive. A review of the proposals that were considered in the House and Senate reveals that one of the specific proposals that was rejected was a draft amendment that limited itself to forbidding Congress from giving preference to one religion over others. In other words, the First Congress considered a nonpreferential version of the First Amendment but declined to adopt it.

Madison introduced the proposed Bill of Rights in the House of Representatives on June 8, 1789.[18] His proposed amendments included one that specified: "The civil rights of none shall be abridged on account of religious belief or worship, nor shall any national religion be established, nor shall the full and equal rights of conscience be in any manner, or on any pretext, infringed." After some debate and modification of the proposed language, the House sent to the Senate a draft version of the religion clauses of the First Amendment that was similar to the version ultimately adopted: "Congress shall make no law establishing religion or prohibiting the free exercise thereof, nor shall the rights of conscience be infringed."

What happened to the language thereafter is important for resolving disputes about the meaning of the First Amendment. Unfortunately, neither the debates in the Senate nor in the subsequent meetings of the House-Senate conference committee were recorded. However, there is a record of the proposals that were considered, and that record is all we need.

The first motion in the Senate presented what today we would call the "no preference" position. The motion was to strike out from the

House proposal "religion, or prohibiting the free exercise thereof," and to insert, "one religious sect or society in preference to others." The motion passed. The proposal on the floor then read: "Congress shall make no law establishing one religious sect or society in preference to others nor shall the rights of conscience be infringed." If this proposal had ultimately carried the day, the nonpreferentialists obviously would have a strong case.

But the proposal did not prevail. The proposed language changed a couple more times, in a rather bewildering fashion. The Senate first broadened the scope of the amendment considerably and then narrowed it almost beyond recognition. First, it accepted a proposal not dissimilar from the final language of the amendment: "Congress shall make no law establishing religion or prohibiting the free exercise thereof." However, a week later, for reasons unknown to us, the Senate changed its mind and produced a version of the amendment that seemed to limit the government's powers over religion only in a few specific areas: "Congress shall make no law establishing articles of faith or a mode of worship, or prohibiting the free exercise of religion." This was the language that was returned to the House, along with Senate versions of the other amendments.

The House agreed to the Senate's language on most of the other amendments but would not accept the Senate's version of the First Amendment, and consequently, a joint conference committee was formed to resolve the differences between the two chambers. The language that emerged from the conference committee was the language that was adopted and eventually ratified. "Congress shall make no law respecting an establishment of religion or prohibiting the free exercise thereof."

There are a couple of noteworthy aspects of this final language. The clause prohibits any law "respecting," that is, regarding or relating to, an establishment of religion. Thus, not just laws that explicitly establish religion are forbidden, but also laws that tend to establish religion, through support or endorsement. In addition, the clause's prohibition is not limited to establishment of *a* religion but rather extends to anything respecting "establishment of religion" in general. That is, a law does not have to favor one particular religion to violate the First Amendment; it merely has to favor religion in general.

Given this legislative history, it is implausible to maintain that the Establishment Clause merely requires the government to be neutral among religions. Congress considered and rejected language that might have allowed for support of religion in general. Therefore, to insist that the First Amendment permits such support is akin to arguing that a proposed sales price for a house is binding on the seller even when that price was explicitly considered and rejected during contract negotiations. As one constitutional scholar has observed, restricting the reach of the Establishment Clause to a prohibition on preferential aid "requires a premise that the Framers were extraordinarily bad drafters—that they believed one thing but adopted language that said something substantially different and that they did so after repeatedly attending to the choice of language."[19]

It only remains to observe that the notion that the First Amendment allows the government to support religious entities, provided it does so on a nonpreferential basis, completely misconceives the relationship between the Bill of Rights and the Constitution. It is undisputed that the underlying purpose of the Bill of Rights is to remove any doubts about the limits of government power with respect to certain fundamental rights. As we have already seen, the Constitution itself grants no authority to the government to interfere in religious matters. So on the nonpreferentialist reading of the First Amendment, the Establishment Clause of the First Amendment *actually expands government powers*. This would make it the only provision in the Bill of Rights that does so.

The only reasonable conclusion is that the First Amendment confirms and fortifies the secular structure of the government of the United States. This is a government with limited powers, all of which relate to civil interests. It has no authority to enact laws relating to religious matters.

Before considering how religion has fared under secular regimes, I will consider one last objection to the claim that the United States is a secular state. This is the objection that the United States is really a Christian nation, not a secular state, and the government has the authority to support Christian religions and base its law on Christian doctrines. In fact, according to some advocates of the Christian nation theory, the American government not only was founded on biblical principles, but it also exists primarily to enforce God's moral law.[20]

Regrettably, Christian nation advocates have had some success in persuading members of the public to accept their thesis, which perhaps says more about many Americans' lack of historical knowledge than it does about their religious predilections. In addition, in some instances, Christian nation advocates have successfully applied pressure on state and local school boards to alter the prescribed program of studies in public schools. Christian nation advocates are a force that must be taken seriously.

For practical political purposes, they must be taken seriously, but at an intellectual level, their arguments are specious, to put it mildly. Were it not for the fact that Christian nation advocates unintentionally make an interesting point about the relations between religious believers and a secular state, their arguments would hardly be worth considering. (I'll get to the interesting point below.) The arguments made by Christian nation advocates are composed of one part irrelevant, cherry-picked factoids and two parts fallacy—and that's when they make factually accurate claims, which, sadly, is not always the case.

For example, Christian nation advocates often point to some early colonial documents such as the Mayflower Compact and the Fundamental Orders of Connecticut. Why? These documents contain various references to God and Christianity. The Fundamental Orders go as far as to assert that Connecticut has been founded in part "to maintain and preserve the liberty and purity of the Gospel of our Lord Jesus."[21] But it is fantasy and fallacy to conclude that the United States—a nation that came into existence about 150 years after these documents were written—has the structure of a Christian nation because of these documents. These documents may have some relevance to the structure of early colonial governments, but the early governments of a couple of colonies are not equivalent to the government of the United States. No one disputes that Massachusetts had a government that was pervasively religious. It was a bloody theocracy—bloody in the literal sense, as we have seen. This type of government, with its persecution of religious minorities, was precisely the type of government the Founders did not want for the new nation.

The document that is most relevant for understanding the structure of our government is, of course, the Constitution. The wording of this document simply does not square with the bizarre thesis of Christian nation advocates. It defies belief to maintain the Founders intended to create a Christian nation, yet they omitted all references to God and Jesus in the Constitution. If the Founders wanted to ensure a government based on Christian precepts, why is not Jesus invoked plainly and repeatedly in the text of the document? At a minimum, Christianity could have received a nod in the Preamble by having the opening clause state "in order to found a more perfect union *based on Christian principles.*" It would not have taken much effort to include these four words. Christian nation advocates want us to believe Christianity was of central importance to the Founders, and they wanted the new nation to be based on Christian principles, but yet they could not be bothered to make reference to it in the Constitution.

Another irrelevant set of facts cited by the Christian nation advocates relates to the religious composition of the early nation as a whole and of the Founders in particular. Books and pamphlets published to support the Christian nation claim are awash with quotations from various members of the founding generation that state or suggest they accepted some form of Christianity. It is further claimed the people of the new nation were almost all Christian. These assertions are partially correct, but also misleading.

Most of the population of the United States at the time of its founding was at least nominally Christian, in fact, Protestant Christian, but using a generic term like "Christian" as the primary descriptive term for their beliefs misrepresents and obscures the religious sensibilities of the time. People considered themselves Congregationalists, Episcopalians, Baptists, Friends (Quakers), Presbyterians, and so forth. Denominational differences among Protestants were more significant than they are now. These serious doctrinal differences between Protestant denominations were one reason it was important for the government to remain out of the religion business. The term "Christian" was used from time to time to distinguish Christianity from Judaism or "infidelity," but it is anachronistic to blend together all the different denominations of the time and attribute to them some unexpressed desire for a "Christian" nation.

What is true of the general population is even more true of the Founders. Many belonged to one Protestant denomination or another, but more than a few were deists or Unitarians, including key Founders such as Jefferson, Franklin, Adams, and Washington. Therefore, it is even less likely that the Founders would have submerged their distinct personal religious beliefs into a homogenous Christian stew and have this jumble serve as the cornerstone of the nation. Such a decision also would have been wholly at odds with the political writings of the Founders, who, time after time, emphasized they accepted the Lockean understanding of the state, with its sharp separation between civil matters, the business of the government, and religious matters, the exclusive province of religious institutions.

James Madison's *Memorial and Remonstrance Against Religious Assessments*, a petition he wrote and disseminated in 1785, perhaps best illustrates the view held by Madison and many other Founders that the government must stay completely out of religious affairs.[22] The context for the pamphlet was a proposal in the Virginia legislature to assess a tax on Virginia citizens that would be used to support ministers and teachers of Christian religions. Madison's petition against the proposed tax argued that it violated the freedom of conscience possessed by each individual by compelling everyone to support religious beliefs, including beliefs with which they may disagree. Only a government that stayed out of religious issues completely could protect religious liberty. In Madison's words, "Religion is wholly exempt from [the] cognizance" of government. On the strength of Madison's petition, the assessment scheme was defeated.

There has been a fair amount of debate about Madison's personal religious beliefs, just as there has been debate about the beliefs of luminaries such as Jefferson and Washington. Some claim he was a devout Episcopalian; others claim he was a deist. The reality is we may never know the exact content of his beliefs because he was very reticent about discussing them—which is fine, because it doesn't really matter.

Not unexpectedly, Christian nation advocates emphasize letters or other writings that suggest Madison was a Christian. But their emphasis on Madison's religiosity, just like the reliance they place on the religious beliefs of Madison's contemporaries, exposes the key fallacy of the Christian nation thesis, which is that being a Christian somehow commits one to the view that the government must be based on biblical precepts. Christian nation proponents make an inference from the premise that Madison, many of the Founders, and much of the population were Christian, to the conclusion that they must have wanted the United States to be structured as a Christian nation. Uh, ... no. Fortunately, the people who established the United States did not suffer from the narrow-mindedness, lack of foresight, and ethical blindness that afflicts many Christian nation advocates. There is no contradiction in being Christian and being in favor of a secular nation. Far from it. People like Madison recognized that freedom of conscience is an important value that Christians should embrace. If Madison was a Christian, he was like many other enlightened Christians of his time; they did not want people pressured, directly or indirectly, into becoming Christians. They thought people should come to Christ of their own free will. Furthermore, they recognized that a secular state, a state that does not have the authority to meddle in religious matters, is the best guarantor of religious liberty, for Christians and for everyone else. A government that believes it has the authority to regard itself as the government of an officially Christian nation, will also think it has the authority to define what beliefs and practices are truly Christian. Some day it may also believe that it has the authority to declare itself the government of an officially Islamic nation or atheist nation.

To sum up: those who were responsible for establishing the American state were persuaded by Locke and other theorists that the proper model for governance was a secular state that would respect certain fundamental human rights and derive its authority from the consent of the governed. Such a secular state would concern itself exclusively with things of this world, not involve itself in religious matters, and treat all its citizens equally regardless of their religious beliefs.

The History of the Secular State and Its Relationship to Religion
No one would argue that life in the United States has been perfectly tranquil and prosperous since 1789 and that we have completely avoided religious bigotry, violent religious clashes, or government-enforced religious discrimination. Of course not. There have been a number of religiously inspired violent episodes, particularly anti-Catholic and anti-Mormon riots in the nineteenth century, and an extensive anti-Semitism that receded significantly only after the Second World War.

One of the groups that most suffered from discrimination were atheists. Moreover, this was *de jure* discrimination, not just *de facto* discrimination. Under the laws of many states, atheists were treated as second-class citizens. Atheists were barred from testifying, serving on juries, and holding public office in most states well into the twentieth century. (Recall that the First Amendment applied only to the federal government, not state governments, until the Supreme Court ruled otherwise in 1940.)[23] De Tocqueville, in *Democracy in America,* relates one particularly shameful episode:

> While I was in America, a witness who happened to be called at the Sessions of the County of Chester (State of New York) declared that he did not believe in the existence of God or in the immortality of the soul. The judge refused to admit his evidence on the ground that the witness had destroyed beforehand all the confidence of the court in what he was about to say. The newspapers related the fact without any further comment.[24]

Not a morally uplifting tale, and it is indicative of the bigotry felt by many toward atheists, not only in the 1800s, but continuing, to some extent, until today. But this bias was, and is, found in many other countries as well. It is a product of ignorance, prejudice, and God-intoxication; it is not a fault peculiar to the secular state.

Despite having an imperfect record, the secular state has not experienced the horrible religious conflicts that convulsed early modern Europe. In fact, the superior record of the secular state has been sufficiently apparent that the majority of nations, at least in the developed world, are now organized either explicitly or implicitly as secular states. (Some nations are effectively secular even though they retain vestiges of an established religion.)

Secular states have not only kept the religious peace, but, arguably, they have been good for the preservation, if not growth, of religious belief. The United States was the first secular state, and no other developed nation has such a strong and extensive community of believers. Again, it is difficult to isolate one or two causes as the explanation for deep, diffuse religious beliefs, but the fact that in the United States people have been free to explore and follow their personal spiritual revelations undoubtedly accounts for some of the robustness of religion in America. Few, if any other, countries have witnessed the invention of so many religions as the United States. The United States has given birth to Adventists, Jehovah's Witnesses, Mormons, Christian Scientists, Pentecostals, and Scientologists, to name just some of the more well-known creeds. Walled off from state regulation by the Constitution, the fertile garden of religious imagination has yielded an incomparable bounty. According to the Gospel of Matthew, whenever two are gathered in Jesus' name, he is among them (Matt. 18: 20). In the United States, whenever at least two individuals are together, you may find a new religion. The secular state is no enemy of religion.

At this point, I suspect some may be thinking: well, what about the state of religion in Communist countries—China, North Korea, Cuba, the then Soviet Union and its satellites? To which I respond: these were not and are not true secular states. Or if that seems like too much of a dodge for you, you can just say these are examples of deformed secular states. Yes, the Communist nations separated religious doctrines and beliefs from the state, but they did not remain neutral between religion and irreligion. Instead, for all practical purposes, they enshrined atheism as the official doctrine of the state. (I say "for all practical purposes" because as a technical legal matter only Albania ever declared itself an atheist state; other Communist countries kept up a facade of neutrality on religious matters.) Again, atheism is not the same as secularism. Making atheism the official belief of the state is just the flip side of making Catholicism or Islam the official belief of the state. It is wrong. It violates freedom of conscience. It also violates the Lockean understanding of a secular state, which removes the government from religious matters entirely. The secular state neither advances nor inhibits religion. It leaves religious issues up to the people. Communist nations have not left religious matters up to the people. To the contrary, these countries have placed a very heavy thumb on the atheist side of the scale. Many Communist countries launched prolonged campaigns against religion, supported by public resources.[25] Persecution of and discrimination against believers were routine. They still are in some countries.

In chapter 1, I mentioned how widespread atheism is a phenomenon of just the last few decades. I'm sure some readers were thinking I was wrong because I was overlooking countries such as the Soviet Union, where the Bolsheviks seized power almost a century ago, in 1917. But the atheism in Communist countries was almost entirely top-down atheism. It was forced on the people. Professions of atheism did not express wholly voluntary decisions, as is the case with contemporary atheism in democratic countries. The fact that professions of atheism in Communist states did not necessarily reflect the genuine beliefs of the populace has been corroborated by the religious revival in many formerly Communist nations, and by the continuing (if not increasing) strength of religious/spiritual beliefs and practices in China.

So do not use the Communist nations as examples of secular states. The Communist nations have paid no more than lip service to the Lockean position that governments must not interfere in religious matters. They have continually suppressed religious beliefs and in doing so have violated a key Lockean precept: governments should not make judgments on theological matters.

That said, Communist nations may be examples of what some believers fear will happen if they lose their dominant position in our culture. With respect to the democratic, developed nations, these fears are groundless. Except for a few cranks, atheists do not want to use force to pressure the religious into abandoning their religious beliefs. Atheists in the democratic world are as firmly committed to freedom of conscience as the majority of believers—they remember that not that long ago they were denied this precious right, so there is no eagerness to give government the power to interfere with religious beliefs.

What then of the claims being made—typically by fundamentalist Christians—of discrimination? Almost all these claims of discrimination lack any substance. All that is happening is that religion is losing some of its former privileged position. Yes, even though we in the United States legally have had a secular state at the federal level since the time of the Constitution, this does not mean the federal government has always been consistent in adhering to the principles of a secular state. More importantly, the guarantee of separation of church and state found in the U.S. Constitution did not apply to state and local governments until the 1940s. Some state and local governments encouraged majoritarian religious beliefs, as indicated by the widespread use of official prayers and Bible readings in public schools, which the Supreme Court did not prohibit until the 1960s. Accordingly, believers in the United States used to take for granted that teachers would lead students in prayer, religious symbols could be placed in prominent positions in public places, textbooks would extol the virtues of religion, and government meetings would open and close with prayers. Some of this mixing of religion and government has stopped, and this has upset many who just assumed this was the accepted and legally permissible way of doing things. They interpret the end of the privileging of religion as discriminatory when in reality it is just religion losing some of its favored status, and of the U.S. Constitution being enforced.

This sense of entitlement is most manifest in an area outside of direct government control, however. Nonetheless, ending the privilege enjoyed by the religious in this area is even more important than ending government's use of religious symbolism. It is a matter of ensuring democracy can function effectively in a society that has a mix of believers and nonbelievers. I am referring to the entitlement many believers feel they have to address and resolve moral issues, and public policy questions involving moral issues, using religious doctrines. Use of religious doctrines in such disputes has the effect of shutting nonbelievers out of the conversation. In such a situation, believer and nonbeliever cannot reason together to find common ground. It is good to have a secular state, but that is no longer sufficient. We need to move to a secular society. The next chapter will show how.

Three

FROM THE SECULAR STATE
TO THE SECULAR SOCIETY

The secular state is one component of secularism, but secularism means more than keeping the government out of religious affairs. In fact, although the term "secular" as a synonym for things of this world, as opposed to religious matters, has been in use for centuries, "secularism" is a term that appears to have been coined only in the 1840s by George Jacob Holyoake, an activist freethinker in the United Kingdom. It is not entirely clear how Holyoake himself defined secularism because, as one scholar has noted, in Holyoake's published work, "he offered up a plethora of definitions."[1] It is clear, however, that Holyoake understood secularism to include more than just the political separation of church and state. He also understood secularism to have ethical implications. In particular, he urged that in reasoning about moral matters, we should use reason and empirical evidence, look to promote human welfare by measurable material means, and avoid the use of theological precepts. Although a freethinker himself, Holyoake studiously avoided arguing that secularism required people to give up belief in God. Our concern should not be an individual's personal beliefs. The realm of personal spirituality is just that: personal. It's no one else's business.

You can believe in Yahweh, the Trinity, Allah, who- or whatever, but don't use religious dogma as a basis for moral judgments, especially in the area of public policy.

The history of the concept of secularism and how it influenced, or failed to influence, either the governing classes or the general population in the United Kingdom and the United States is an interesting story in and of itself, but it's not what I'll be discussing here. Instead, I want to argue that something like Holyoake's idea of secularism is what both believer and nonbeliever should embrace, if we are to live together as equal citizens in a democracy. We need not just a secular state, but a secular society.

The Prerequisites for Democratic Discourse
Governments derive their authority from the consent of the governed. We elect legislators who are granted the power to enact laws that regulate our lives. In theory, these are laws we are imposing on ourselves. True, it is the majority (or plurality) of voters who decides which legislators are elected, so many people are denied their choice of representative, but at least those in the minority have the opportunity to be heard.

Furthermore—ideally—the competing candidates discuss and debate the policy issues that are of concern to voters. The voters themselves will become informed about these issues and will consider and discuss these issues in private conversations and in various public forums.

And the discussion does not stop once an election is over. As important issues arise, legislators seek input from voters, and the voters analyze and argue about these issues and communicate their views to their legislators. Debates in the legislature take place in the context of public deliberation.

This model is not an entirely accurate representation of the political world, of course. (How's that for an understatement?) Anyone with an ounce of real-world experience knows that many voters are apathetic or ill-informed, the choice among candidates is usually a choice among individuals selected by political parties, which are themselves remote from the influence of most people, "debates" on the issues are condensed into thirty-second political ads or even shorter sound bites, and legislators are more responsive to the special interest groups and corporations that fund their campaigns than they are to the voice of the people. But *some* people do take their civic responsibilities seriously, take steps to educate themselves about the issues, and attempt to engage their fellow citizens in thoughtful discussions. Moreover, legislators are not completely unresponsive to public opinion. Meaningful democratic discourse remains a possibility.

But apart from voter passivity or legislators' disdain for the public, there is another obstacle to meaningful democratic discourse. It's the use of religious doctrine in policy discussions. There are prerequisites for democratic discourse to be successful: people must be willing to discuss the issues, provide reasons for their views, and be open to persuasion; and, in addition, the participants in the discussion must be able to analyze, evaluate, and debate the reasons that others offer for their views. In other words, there must be a commitment to reason together in terms everyone can understand. That is not possible if religious doctrines are offered as a justification for public policy positions—not in a country that is religiously pluralistic and includes a significant number of nonbelievers.

Invoking religious doctrine as justification for public policy silences all those who do not accept those doctrines. For example, if someone opposes legalization of same-sex marriage on the grounds that sexual intercourse between men violates some prohibition in the Old Testament, there is really nothing to say to that person, is there? He has invoked his faith and the conversation is over. As the philosopher and social critic Richard Rorty observed, "in political discussion [religion] is a conversation-stopper."[2]

This is not just a problem with those who are on the conservative side of the political spectrum, although the Religious Right has been more visible in their use of religious doctrine. Left-wing believers use religion as well. Many who want to abolish capital punishment do so because their faith informs them that life is sacred and God has instructed us not to kill. Again, if this is the basis for someone's public policy position, there is no room for debate. Bringing God in shuts down any meaningful debate.

Reliance on religious doctrine often means reliance on citations to scripture. When this happens, reason takes a holiday. A policy discussion turns into a game of "Who has the best quote from scripture?" as participants scramble to mine their memory for a passage from the Bible or Qur'an that supports their position. Extra points are awarded for creatively interpreting a passage that seems adverse to one's position.

Two examples illustrate this reduction of policy debates to scripture-quoting contests. In early 2013, Ralph Reed wrote an article on immigration policy for *USA Today* in which, among other things, he argued against amnesty for illegal aliens based on verses from the Old Testament.[3] Amnesty for illegal aliens may or may not be good policy, but that cannot be resolved by playing the scripture game. Yet this is what Reed urged us to do, ending his article by counseling politicians that if they want to solve the immigration issue they should "sit down with the faith community and perhaps open their Bibles." Reed did not discuss what happens when they open their Bibles to different pages.

The second example is a book that explicitly addresses the proper approach of evangelical Christians to public policy. Entitled *Is the Good Book Good Enough?*, the essays in this volume provide a qualified "yes" to this question.[4] The book is to be applauded for leaving no doubt about the importance of the Bible for informing the evangelical position on public policy matters:

[F]or evangelicals the Bible is God's revelation and the source of authority trumping all else. ... Hence, evangelicals are likely to examine scripture on multiple levels; they read scripture for broad ethical or moral principles while at the same time combing the text for particular commands and instructions (including public policy). Ethical and political cues are to be found in both the general and the special revelation of scripture.[5]

True to this description of the evangelical understanding of the role of religion in public policy, the book provides religious prescriptions for issues as diverse as regulating Wall Street, protection of the environment, and reform of the criminal justice system, with many of the essays studded with scriptural citations. The problem is that whatever the merit of the various positions advanced, the arguments themselves will not engage anyone who does not share the theological commitments of the authors. (To their credit, a couple of the authors recognize this problem.)[6]

Appeals to religious doctrine are inconsistent with democratic discourse. Such appeals are also in tension with at least one aspect of the underlying rationale for a secular state. As we have seen, in the secular state, religious matters are kept distinct from the sphere of government. This limitation on the powers of government acknowledges that the state is not competent to adjudicate religious disputes. Yet if citizens are basing their public policy positions on religious doctrine, they are attempting to impose their religious views on others via the state. Even if they do not succeed in having their positions enacted into law, they are implicitly rejecting the concept of a secular state by attempting to have public policy incorporate their religious views.

The Supreme Court has recognized that using religion in formulating laws is, in some cases, unconstitutional. In the seminal case of *Lemon v. Kurtzman,*[7] the Court set forth a tripartite test for assessing the constitutionality of government action. A law is unconstitutional if it does not have a secular purpose, or if it has the primary effect of advancing or inhibiting religion, or if it fosters excessive government entanglement with religion. The secular purpose prong of this test invalidates government action that is unmistakably designed to promote religion.

However, the problem I am addressing here cannot be resolved by appealing to constitutional law. The secular purpose test focuses on legislative outcomes instead of the public debate surrounding proposed laws or policies. Furthermore, the secular purpose test is fairly easy to circumvent. As long as some plausible secular basis exists for a law or regulation, the Court will not regard it as having violated the secular purpose test. In only a handful of cases has the Court struck down a law on the ground that it lacked a secular purpose, and in those instances the intent to further religion was undeniable (for example, a law prohibiting the teaching of evolution).[8] The secular purpose test is important for confirming the fundamental principle that the government cannot enforce religious doctrines through its laws and for guarding against the most egregious efforts to violate this principle—but it cannot be used effectively to regulate discourse about proposed laws and regulations.

We cannot codify into law a commitment to democratic discourse that ensures religious considerations are kept out of policy discussions—nor, because of the importance of protecting free speech, should we even think of doing so. To keep religious doctrine out of democratic discourse, we have to appeal to the believer's prudence, self-interest, commitment to democracy, and moral sensibilities. Prudence, because in a religiously diverse society we are not going to make any progress in discussions about public policy if people allow their religious beliefs to dictate their positions. Self-interest, because if religion is permitted to influence our discussions about public policy, then the religious beliefs that attract the most adherents will prevail. When the population of the United States was overwhelmingly mainline Protestant, perhaps this did not seem much of a problem because the differences in beliefs, at least with respect to policy issues, were manageable. Increasing diversity has made consensus on some issues more difficult, however, as indicated by the sharp disagreements among religious adherents on issues such as contraception, abortion, and same-sex marriage. If Islam grows in numbers in the next few decades, differences based on religious dogma will likely become even more pronounced. Do believers want public policy determined by which creed can mobilize the most voters?

Cutting short meaningful discussion of public policy by reliance on one's religious beliefs also shows a lack of respect for the equal standing of the citizens who don't share one's beliefs. For all practical purposes, a religiously based public policy claim can be evaluated only through the theology peculiar to the religion of the proponent of the claim. No one can assess that claim without adopting the proponent's religious point of view and sectarian religious vocabulary. Using your religious beliefs as a basis for a policy argument is like using a private language that's intelligible only to your coreligionists. The common language that's accessible to everyone is, of course, language that describes all aspects of issues—the problems, the proposed solutions, our objectives and goals—in secular terms. Formulating one's public policy arguments in secular terms is necessary to engage all of one's fellow citizens. If all you're doing in a discussion on public policy is preaching your own religious doctrines, you might as well shut up and just use your Bible or Qur'an as a bludgeon. Your message is: accept my religious doctrines; accept my religious doctrines; accept my religious doctrines.

Finally, refraining from interjecting religious doctrine into public policy debates displays both an intellectual openness and a sense of moral responsibility that is praiseworthy. In being willing to discuss the secular considerations in favor of a position, a believer indicates both that she is not so arrogant to think she can read the mind of God and that she takes responsibility for coming to her own conclusions about moral issues. (These are important points, and I will expand upon them later.)

My thesis, that discourse about public policy should be framed entirely in secular terms, and decisions about public policy should be based entirely on secular considerations, is foreshadowed in the work of some well-known political philosophers, such as John Rawls and Bruce Ackerman and, as already indicated, the philosopher and social critic Richard Rorty.[9] In his magisterial work, *A Theory of Justice*, Rawls maintained that when people discuss policy questions, particularly policy questions that relate to limitations on liberty of conscience, "ways of reasoning" about such matters "should be of a kind everyone can recognize."[10] Furthermore, the reasoning "must be supported by ordinary observation and modes of thought (including the methods of rational scientific inquiry where these are not controversial) which are generally recognized as correct."[11] For Rawls, this limitation on the contents of democratic discourse "represents an agreement to limit liberty only by reference to a common knowledge and understanding of the world" and does not infringe "anyone's equal freedom."[12] Rawls was more explicit about these points in his later work, *Political Liberalism*, in which he argued that in public policy deliberations, we should "appeal only to presently accepted general beliefs and forms of reasoning found in common sense, and the methods and conclusions of science when these are not controversial."[13] Ackerman, in *Social Justice in the Liberal State,* concurs, forcefully arguing for the exclusion of religious content from public policy discussions. According to Ackerman, no one "has the right to vindicate political authority by asserting a privileged insight into the moral universe which is denied the rest of us."[14] For example, when one discusses restrictions on abortion, no one can advance an argument "on the basis of some conversation with the spirit world."[15]

It would be misleading to leave the impression, however, that there is no dissent within the scholarly community from the proposition that religious beliefs should not be invoked in public policy discussions. There have been various counterarguments to the secular stance. Many of these counterarguments have focused on one key premise of my argument—namely, that invoking religious doctrine effectively stops all meaningful discussion. You might ask, why is it the case that reliance on religion cuts short discussion? Can't we discuss someone's religiously based positions just like we discuss other beliefs? Some scholars have made this claim, including Jeffrey Stout and J. Caleb Clanton.[16] Stout contends we *can* argue with those who use religious doctrine provided we accept, for purposes of argument, their perspective. Stout advocates the use of "immanent criticism," by which he means arguing from within the framework of your opponent. With immanent criticism, those engaged in public policy discussion "either try to show that their opponents' views are incoherent, or they try to argue positively from their opponents' religious premises to the conclusion that the proposal [in question] is acceptable."[17] Clanton's view is similar to Stout's except that he criticizes Stout for retaining a prudential constraint on public policy deliberations—namely, that all participants in the discussion should aim at convincing others and tailor their reasoning accordingly. Clanton sees public policy discourse as serving, at least on occasion, a "Socratic" function, that is, it does not necessarily function as a means of resolving disagreements but of clarifying values.[18]

Can we have public policy discussions in which religious claims are meaningfully debated? In theory, perhaps; in reality, no. Stout's advice to adopt the perspective of the believer and argue against the believer based on the implications of the believer's own premises assumes that the believer is constrained by the standards of logic and evidence that apply to secular arguments. However, religious belief is not something usually held to the same standards of consistency, rationality, and evidential support as are other beliefs on which public policy might be based, and that includes our moral beliefs. Interpretation of scripture is not a science, and there is no logical compulsion for a believer to prefer one interpretation over another. Similarly, with respect to core religious doctrines, whether ethical or metaphysical, the use of reason is severely restricted. Stout suggests that the believer would balk at internal inconsistencies within his positions. But believers do not necessarily feel they must resolve apparent contradictions. What seems an inconsistency to those outside the faith tradition may seem to be reconcilable propositions or a divine "mystery" to those within the faith tradition. Consider a central doctrine of the Christian faith, namely, the Incarnation. That Jesus was both divine and human seems on the face of it impossible—it's a transparent contradiction to claim Jesus was simultaneously a person with limited powers and a deity with unlimited powers—but that does not prevent Christians from asserting this belief because at the end of the day they can always invoke "faith." "Faith" means not having to supply reasons. Hebrews 11:1 (faith is the conviction of things not seen). Once a person pulls out the faith card, they have a free pass (or at least they think they're entitled to a free pass). You cannot argue with someone's faith.

Furthermore, even if adherents of a religion were willing to allow their beliefs to be examined critically—and certainly *some* believers are willing to submit at least *some* of their claims to scrutiny—think about how incredibly involved the process of determining public policy could become. Every time someone offered a religious belief as a justification for public policy, we could become immersed in a complex discussion about whether the belief has the implications the believer thinks it has and, ultimately, whether the underlying religious belief is justified. Let's say there's a dispute about the best educational method to reduce STDs among teens and teen pregnancy. Some Christians favor funding abstinence-only education because according to them fornication is a sin, and they have some scriptural citations to support them. For non-Christians even to begin a discussion within the framework of the believers, they would need to spend a considerable amount of time studying Christian doctrine and reviewing scripture. ("Want to debate abstinence-only education? OK, but hold on: I'll get back to you next month after I train myself to argue from within your perspective.")

Once the non-Christian feels adequately prepared, she could try to engage the believer by arguing about the implications of scripture. This requires exegesis of biblical texts that are not terribly straightforward or transparent in their meaning. One could easily spend a few hours going back-and-forth about whether Jesus actually condemned fornication—but why waste one's time? It's illusory to think we can shake the believer's confidence in his claim that fornication is condemned. There's no unambiguous passage from the New Testament indicating Jesus had no objection to it (is there any unambiguous passage in the New Testament on anything?), and, anyway, the believer has no obligation to give up his preferred interpretation of the relevant verses.

Perhaps we could then try to take the dispute to the next level. We could ask whether, even assuming there is a God and Jesus is divine, we should accept the books of the New Testament as the exclusive source of Jesus' teachings. We now know, for example, that the four canonical gospels set forth in the New Testament represent a fraction of the various gospels regarding Jesus that floated around in the first few centuries of the Common Era. How do we determine which statements attributed to Jesus actually represent the views of Jesus? These are not questions that can be resolved, if at all, within the context of a time-limited public policy discussion. Scholars have spent decades on such questions. Indeed, scholars are not even in agreement on whether Jesus was an actual historical figure.[19]

It is, perhaps, technically true that immanent criticism can prevent religion from being a conversation-stopper. But in trying to fulfill its goal of keeping the conversation going, it creates the opposite problem: the conversation *never* stops. Immanent criticism, in many cases, would lead nowhere but to interminable debate. Furthermore, although understanding the perspective of others is all well and good, we do not have the luxury of placing policy questions on hold while everyone pursues a degree in comparative religion. Clanton, to his credit, recognizes the problem of what he labels "deliberative stalemate" that might result from introducing religious beliefs into public debates. He proposes that in such an instance we resort to a temporary *modus vivendi*, in which a temporary policy is crafted by "weigh[ing] the competing interests on all deliberative sides, and try[ing] to gerrymander some sort of policy which is maximally sensitive to as many interests as possible." One's immediate reaction to this proposal is "Good luck with that." "Maximally sensitive to as many interests as possible" in the real world will translate as "maximally sensitive to whoever has the most power." Political pressure, divided along religious lines, will substitute for democratic discourse. Moreover, we need to ask why we should hold progress on public policy matters hostage to religious groups who are unwilling to discuss and defend their positions in terms everyone can understand and evaluate.

Despite the counterarguments of Stout, Clanton, and others, introducing religious beliefs into policy discussions inevitably throws a monkey wrench into such discussions. If the discussion doesn't stop completely, it gets thrown off course and derailed into ultimately unproductive theological disputes. In addition, such discussions are bound to exacerbate the tensions between different religious groups and between believer and nonbeliever. As George Washington observed, "Religious controversies are always productive of more acrimony and irreconcilable hatreds than those which spring from any other cause."[20] In recent years, there has been much hand-wringing over the supposedly abrasive rhetoric of the "New Atheists"—various scholars and writers who have not hesitated to point out some of the contradictions and apparent absurdities in many religious beliefs. Feelings have been hurt. Anger has ensued. However, one could avoid exposure to the New Atheists just by not buying their books and otherwise not paying attention to them. That simple expedient will not be possible if we have religion as an integral part of any policy debate that touches on moral issues. If some people are going to be relying on God's word, each discussion of policy will threaten to turn into an acrimonious debate about the meaning of God's word, whose God we should rely upon, and whether God even exists. I'm not sure if religion poisons everything, but it does corrupt discussion of public policy.

Contrast this religion-laden approach to public policy with the secular approach. Consider the example I used before, that is, the policy question of whether abstinence-only courses should be funded. As indicated, the primary goals of the proposed educational program are to reduce STDs and unwanted pregnancy. If abstinence-only education is effective in achieving these goals, especially if it is more effective than standard sex education, perhaps it should be supported. If it is not, then support may not be advisable. This is a question that can be resolved through empirical studies—studies that are set forth in language that everyone, at least in principle, can understand. Granted these empirical studies cannot be done overnight, but they require a finite amount of time and yield clear results, as contrasted with the lifetime of study that would be required to address abstruse theological questions that do not promise to yield a definitive answer *ever*.

A secular society, a society in which there is general recognition that the public realm is concerned exclusively with this-worldly and not otherworldly matters, is the only way in which a religiously diverse nation can function effectively. When entering the public square to discuss matters of common concern, everyone must use a common—that is, secular—language. Revelations from spiritual sources must be left at home.

I previously stated that keeping religious doctrines out of democratic discourse depends largely on the voluntary actions of believers. That is correct. We certainly do not want legal restrictions on what private individuals say during public policy discussions. There is a particular group of individuals, though, that deserves special attention because of their distinctive ability to limit the intrusion of religious doctrines into policy discussions, and that is legislators and other government officials.

Although it doesn't happen too often, occasionally Congress or some government agency or advisory commission holds hearings on proposed legislation or regulations and "expert" witnesses are called in from various religious denominations. They are there to discuss the ethical aspects of the legislation or regulation from the perspective of their faith tradition. Why? Their testimony does not serve any legitimate purpose. Either their testimony has no influence on the legislators or regulators and their presence is simply being exploited for political purpose or their testimony does have an influence and we have religious doctrine shaping public policy. The former is manipulation of religion by the government; the latter is intrusion of religion into government. Either outcome violates the principles of a secular society.

There is absolutely nothing wrong with Congress or other governmental bodies requesting the input of individuals with specialized knowledge that might be relevant to proposed legislation or regulation, including situations where the government action under consideration has moral implications. To the contrary, seeking such advice is both laudable and prudent. Depending on the issue in question, economists, physicians, molecular biologists, sociologists, and so forth may have information that should be considered. But theologians or other representatives of religious bodies? What can they possibly say that would be relevant to anyone outside of their particular faith tradition? Of course, the pretext usually given for inviting theologians or clergy is that they will be able to provide a moral perspective on the issues. This privileging of religion with respect to moral issues has no justification other than the folk belief that religion provides the foundation for morality. We need to put an end to this unthinking equation of religion with morality. It has no basis in logic or fact. As I have stated, it is undeniable that religious institutions have played a significant role in inculcating morality. However, this does not imply that religious doctrines are necessary or sufficient for morality, much less that one cannot be a moral person without believing in God. (The middle chapters of this book will establish that morality is not dependent on God.)

A recent example of a congressional committee's reliance on testimony from religious representatives was the January 2014 hearing held by the House Subcommittee on the Constitution. The current and former lobbyists for the United States Conference of Catholic Bishops were invited to testify on proposed anti-abortion legislation. They had no legitimate reason for being there. The hearing degenerated into a discussion of Pope Francis's view on income inequality and whether eliminating poverty was now more a priority for the Catholic Church than combatting abortion.[21] The views of Pope Francis, whether laudable or lamentable, have no relevance to the legislation of a secular state.

The use of theological experts by Congress or other governmental bodies is not made any more acceptable if representatives of various faiths are invited (current standard lists of invitees: Catholic, Protestant, Jew, Muslim) to avoid the appearance that the government is favoring one religion. This attempt at even-handedness just underscores the futility and pointlessness of the practice. The result is self-proclaimed interpreters of God's words expressing disagreement about the meaning of God's words. For a representative democracy in the twenty-first century, such an exhibition is disgraceful. It succeeds only in degrading both government and religion.

The worst example of this practice may have been the invitation to testify extended to various theologians by President Bill Clinton's National Bioethics Advisory Commission when the commission was considering the issue of human cloning.[22] Cloning? The Tanakh, the New Testament, and the Qur'an have absolutely nothing to say about this topic, but that did not prevent the invited scholars from waxing eloquent about God's views on the issue. All they wound up contributing were dogmatic pronouncements without any support external to their own religious tradition. Oh, and the Catholic God was strongly against cloning while the Jewish God permitted cloning if necessary to preserve a person's genetic line. Identifying the right policy all depends on which God you listen to.

I choose the testimony of religious leaders on cloning as an example because it illustrates nicely the senselessness of using religious teachings as guidance on contemporary moral issues. Three major religions—Judaism, Christianity and Islam—base their ethical views on teachings that were committed to writing from around 700 BCE to 700 CE. Given the limits of their world, the authors of these sacred scriptures simply had no occasion to address some of today's issues, such as stem cell research, in vitro fertilization, genetic engineering, organ transplantation, or cloning. (Even scriptures written or "discovered" closer in time—such as the Book of Mormon—could not anticipate these issues. The world has changed a lot in the last fifty years.) To pretend otherwise, and to try to apply ancient religious precepts by extension and analogy to these modern moral problems, is an act of folly. Religious teachings have no place in public policy discussions.

But will sufficient people heed this advice for it to be effective? There are grounds for optimism. Many religious people already accept the secular boundaries of democratic discourse —with no ill effects to their religious beliefs, by the way. On the other hand, perhaps in a country such as the United States, in which religious groups have had substantial success in influencing public policy, the advice to adhere to the limits of meaningful democratic discourse will be ignored by a preponderance of believers. In this case, we will have increasingly divisive discussions about policy matters. I am not even sure we could call them discussions, because people will be talking past each other, not talking with each other.

This would be a very bad outcome for everyone. We need to engage with each other. Make no mistake—I want the participation of believers in policy discussions. Nothing I have said should be interpreted as a call to exclude believers from our public forums. To the contrary, not only do they have a right to participate, but they should participate. A representative democracy should hear from all the people. What I am urging is that believers frame their claims in secular terms and base their arguments on secular considerations. That is, I am urging they talk in terms everyone can understand.

One hesitation that some believers may have about honoring the secular boundaries of democratic discourse is their sense that keeping their religious beliefs private implies that relevant moral considerations will be kept out of public policy discussions. If morality were based on religion, then my recommendation to keep religious beliefs out of policy discussions would also be a prescription for eliminating moral considerations from policy discussions. This would be neither desirable nor possible. But morality is *not* based on religion, and at least some of the reasoning in which many religious people engage reflects that fact. Furthermore, as demonstrated in the next chapters, we share a common morality that can be articulated in secular terms and which, in combination with relevant facts, can provide a basis for moral judgments.

Before we address these issues, however, we need to consider an objection by some that asking religious individuals to "restructure their arguments in purely secular terms before they can be presented" in public forums is "unsatisfying and even demeaning" to many religious people.[23]

Secular Discourse: Does It Ask Too Much of the Religious?

I have already discussed the objections of scholars like Stout, who claim that religious precepts can be incorporated into policy discussions with no significant adverse effect. There is a distinct set of objections, however, that focuses more on the silencing of believers that supposedly results from limiting democratic discourse to secular concerns. Several authors have made this point, including Michael Perry, Noah Feldman, and Stephen Carter. For example, Feldman writes: "In a society in which some citizens base their political choices on deeply held religious beliefs, requiring political discourse to be secular systematically excludes them from the political conversation."[24] Carter is especially emphatic on this point: "the effort to place limits [on religious considerations] is less likely to move many citizens to restructure their arguments than to silence them—or, perhaps ... to move them to revolution."[25]

As already indicated, I certainly don't want to silence religious believers, although, because I want to be able to talk with them and not listen to stories about revelations from an invisible world, I do want them to present their arguments in accessible, secular terms. Contrary to what Feldman, Perry, and Carter suggest, this is not an onerous burden. Most believers, like everyone else, live day-to-day in a secular world, a world in which we have no trouble communicating about natural phenomena. Commuting to work, carrying out one's tasks in conjunction with colleagues, consulting with one's physician, buying groceries, and so forth are all done—typically—via entirely secular transactions. Everyone understands secular terminology and knows how to discuss cause and effect and logical relationships in secular terms. You don't need a Bible to conclude that *if all humans are mortal, and Socrates is human, then Socrates is mortal.* So secular language is spoken by believers already; they just have to apply it to public policy issues.

But morality is different, the believer will claim. We need to refer to religious beliefs in discussing policy questions with moral implications because morality is based on God's commands, which we know through revelation.

A fuller response to this claim will have to await the next chapter, but for now my response to the believer is to ask, what would God want you to do in talking with your fellow citizens: talk *at* them using verbiage that to them is meaningless, or talk *with* them in terms they can understand? Restricting policy discussions to secular arguments, with the consequence that religious claims must be restructured in secular terms, requires some effort by the believer, that is true. But this effort is worthwhile. It can cause one to think. That's a good thing. Moreover, it operates as a much-needed check on the soundness of one's reasoning. If one cannot reformulate a religiously based moral belief in terms that a nonbeliever might find persuasive, one should pause to consider whether one's views are correct. Perhaps you have misinterpreted God's commandments. After all, why would God ask you to follow a rule that does not make any sense when you try to explain it to someone else? Secularizing one's moral judgments is a good exercise for the believer, providing him with the opportunity to consider and analyze his moral commitments.

Sure, it's easier, and therefore tempting, not to go through this process. I mean no disrespect for the believer in noting that the relative lack of effort that's required to follow religiously based moral rules is one advantage that religion has over secular systems of thought. For the believer, there's often a set of commandments that one has memorized. If these don't fit one's situation exactly, you can listen to what your priest, minister, rabbi, or imam says. Internet access now facilitates this.[26] If you're really perplexed, perhaps you'll open the Bible, read what you think is a relevant passage, and, after some reflection, "hear" God talk to you.

John Locke (yes, he covered a lot of ground) noted this temptation to shrug off the burden of reasoning and to rely instead on some revelation from God, and warned against it:

> Immediate revelation being a much easier way for men to establish their opinions and regulate their conduct, than the tedious and not always successful labor of strict reasoning, it is no wonder, that some have been very apt to pretend to revelation, and to persuade themselves that they are under the peculiar guidance of heaven in their actions and opinions, especially in those of them which they cannot

account for by the ordinary methods of knowledge, and principles of reason.[27]

The reformulation of religious convictions into secular arguments not only allows the religious person to communicate with those who don't share her faith, but it also provides some assurance to the believer that her "sense" of what is right is correct. A revelation that cannot be supported by secular considerations is questionable. Is that God or the devil talking? As Locke noted elsewhere in this same work, "*Reason must be our last judge and guide in everything.*"[28]

Against this, Carter doggedly maintains that for the believer the will of God must remain the touchstone; God is the only legitimate authority for settling moral disputes.[29] Carter also maintains that excluding religiously motivated arguments from public policy debates will somehow impoverish policy debates because religious conviction can "fire the human imagination, and often the conscience, even of nonbelievers."[30]

But Carter offers no way to determine the will of God except by consulting scripture and engaging in prayerful consideration. These methods have not been successful in achieving a moral consensus on any issue, and remain completely inaccessible to both nonbelievers and those believers who don't share the same sacred texts. An anecdote Carter relates unintentionally reveals the serious limitations of determining God's will by consulting scripture aided by prayer. Carter tells how he came to the conclusion that women could be priests within the Episcopal Church. He prayed about it and engaged in what those unsympathetic to his view might call a strained interpretation of the Bible. (The apostle Paul's instruction that women should be silent in the churches and subordinate to men—see 1 Cor. 14:33–35—is dismissed by Carter as not precluding women priests because one must "distinguish between Paul's statements of doctrine and Paul's statements of advice."[31]) Obviously, as Carter recognizes, those who opposed the ordination of women went through the same process of consulting scripture and praying. So who's right? Who knows? There is no way to resolve this dispute through the resources utilized by Carter.

The ordination of women priests in the Episcopal Church is a matter for that religious body. It's not an issue of public policy. But Carter has no alternative resources to offer the believer when he enters the public square to debate policy issues, and not surprisingly when one surveys the various public policy debates into which believers have injected religious doctrine one finds they can be found on all sides of any given issue. Recognition of this fact makes Carter's repeated references to the role of churches within the civil rights movement of the 1950s and 1960s very poignant. Clearly, he thinks this is a significant factor in favor of his argument, proclaiming that "liberal philosophy's distaste for explicit religious argument in the public square cannot accommodate the openly and unashamedly religious rhetoric of the nonviolent civil rights movement."[32] Carter neglects to mention there were a number of churches—black churches—that stood on the sidelines, and a large number of white churches, particularly Southern Baptist congregations, which actively opposed integration.[33] They all used the same Bible. They all prayed. They all employed "unashamedly religious rhetoric." Contrary to Carter, a secular philosophy *can* accommodate all these disputants shouting their contradictory religious slogans by telling them their rhetoric cancels each other out and it would be preferable if they actually engaged each other in a reasoned debate. Religious rhetoric doesn't persuade; it only resonates with those who are predisposed to endorse the position being advocated. Citations to scripture or some other religious authority serve as a makeweight, legitimizing the opinions one already holds.

It's high time to discard the notion that sacred texts provide a clear message on moral issues, even assuming we could all agree on which text was *the* truly sacred one. Let's just consider the Bible, which is the text with which I am most familiar (although I'm fairly certain my observations would apply equally to the Qur'an). The Bible is a lengthy hodgepodge of writings from different periods of time and different authors addressing different subjects. For a text that is supposed to transmit God's guidance to us, it is remarkably obscure, not to say contradictory. This allows those advocating a position to cherry-pick whatever passage they deem helpful—and if the apparent literal meaning doesn't lend itself readily to a favorable interpretation, you can always appeal to its symbolic or allegorical meaning. As a source of moral authority, the Bible is infinitely malleable, which is another way of saying it's useless. *Anything* can be justified through the Bible. (In fact, here's a challenge: pick any proposition you want, give me twenty-four hours, and I will find a passage to support it.)

Don't think so? Here are some of the policy positions that have been justified based on the Bible, along with some of the relevant supporting citations:

Slavery is permissible: Exod. 21:1–11, 20–21 (discussing various instructions pertaining to the treatment of slaves, and affirming that "the slave is [the master's] money"); Philem. *passim* (the entire text deals with Paul's return of a runaway slave to his master); 1 Pet. 2:18–21 (advising slaves to accept punishment, even from an unjust master). Of course, it's significant that Jesus nowhere condemns slavery, despite the ubiquity of the practice.

We should persecute and kill witches aka sorcerers. Exod. 22:18 (don't allow a witch to live); Lev. 20:6 (condemnation of wizards); Deut. 18: 10–11 (don't allow sorcerers or wizards to live among you). Based on such passages tens of thousands of people have been killed, especially during the witch craze in early modern Europe.

We should persecute Jews. Matt. 27:24–26 (crowd of Jews gathered before Pilate shout that Jesus' blood should "be on us and our children"); John 7:1 (indicating Jesus was wary of walking among the Jews of Judea because they sought to kill him); 1 Thess. 2:14–15 (Jews killed Jesus and "displease God and oppose all men"). Persecution of Jews was a recurrent phenomenon in many Christian countries up until recent times. Martin Luther, that great Christian theologian, was a virulent anti-Semite. His 1543 tract, *On the Jews and Their Lies*—nauseating in its hatred—advocated the burning of Jewish homes and synagogues and the forced concentration of Jews under one roof.[34]

Women should not be allowed to vote. 1 Tim. 2:12–14 (women should not have "authority over men"); Eph. 5: 22–24 (wives to be subject to husbands in everything); 1 Cor. 14:34–35 (if women want to know anything, they can ask their husbands at home).

Contraception should be outlawed. Gen. 38: 7–10 (the story of Onan, who let his semen fall on the ground rather than ejaculate inside his dead brother's wife; God then killed him).

The law should prohibit oral sex. Same Onan story (rationale: lawful sex acts have to be open to procreation).

The law should prohibit genetically modified plants. Same Onan story (rationale: we should not permit "unnatural" seed to fall on the ground).

OK, I made the last one up, in the sense that I have never seen the story of Onan used in an argument against genetically modified plants—but it easily could be.

There's no need to belabor this point. Choose *any* position you like and you can find a Bible passage that, with appropriate spin, can be used to support your position.

Carter's claim that religious rhetoric can "fire the human imagination … even of nonbelievers" is accurate. Rhetoric can motivate, and even an atheist could be stirred by a passionate speech that contains religious references. But, as indicated by our brief Bible study, whether religious rhetoric motivates people to adopt good and wise policies is another question. Therefore, it's questionable whether we should encourage people to make policy arguments in religious terms just because such rhetoric might fire our imagination.

There's one last point to address in answering the objections of those who think that excluding religious considerations from the public square in some way adversely affects believers, and it's connected to Carter's remarks about motivation. It's important to emphasize that nothing I have said here implies that religious people shouldn't rely on their beliefs, including their sacred texts, for inspiration. To begin, it would be pointless to insist that people not be inspired by the Bible, the Qur'an, or any other text they find meaningful. If a person is religious, obviously they are going to be inspired by the texts of their religion. Secondly, there's nothing inherently objectionable in people being inspired to undertake action on certain issues based on their reading of the Bible or other sacred texts any more than it's inherently objectionable for someone to be moved to rectify injustice because of some passage in Homer or Shakespeare. Moving people out of their apathy is, almost always, a good thing. It's at the point where one starts to channel one's energies into concrete positions and actions that secular considerations must take over.

What I have been urging in this chapter is that when religious believers do enter the public square to discuss policy matters, they commit to fully engaging in democratic discourse. To do so, they must use our common language, that is, the language of secularism. Advocating for a position based on religious precepts is ineffective, undermines the foundations of democracy, and manifests a lack of respect for one's fellow citizens.

* * * *

Throughout this chapter, I have alluded to one difficulty in secularizing our democratic discourse, and that is the belief that religion provides an indispensable foundation for morality. If religion were indispensable for morality, then it would be impossible to separate completely discussion of moral issues from religious beliefs, and any public policy dispute that involved moral issues would necessarily implicate religious doctrines. I have claimed that we can discuss morality without involving religion, and that we have a base of shared values that allows us to do so. Moreover, I promised I would provide arguments to support that claim. It's time to deliver on that promise.

Four

WHY GOD CAN'T TELL US WHAT TO DO

Many religious people cling tenaciously to the belief that God provides an indispensable foundation for morality. However, when one probes this belief, it's not always clear what the precise content of this belief is. There are at least a couple of distinct ways in which there can be a relationship between God and morality. (Later, I'll analyze four different ways God may relate to morality, but to introduce the problem, I'll just stick with two for now.) One way is a logical connection between God and morality, that is, God—and only God—can determine what's right and what's wrong. If this connection exists, it exists for both the believer and nonbeliever. In other words, morality is based on God's commandments, whether or not atheists recognize this.

Another alleged relationship between God and morality is really a relationship between belief in God and moral behavior. Many maintain that belief in God motivates people to behave morally, or at least more morally than they would otherwise. Put simply, people need to believe in God to be good. Often, this alleged connection between belief in God and moral behavior is based on the presumption that people will not do the right thing unless they think there is an omniscient God

74

who stands ready to punish them for misconduct and reward them for good behavior. This presumption—actually a prejudice—has been around for a long time. As we saw in chapter 2, Locke did not extend toleration to atheists because, in his view, they could not be trusted to keep promises. This prejudice is still prevalent in much of the world, including the United States. A 2007 survey by the Pew Research Center determined that a startling 57 percent of Americans think it is necessary to believe in God in order to be moral.[1] It could be worse. In countries such as Egypt, the percentage of individuals who believe moral conduct requires a belief in God exceeds 90 percent.[2]

I've referred to this belief as a prejudice because there is no empirical evidence to support the belief that atheists, as a class, are immoral, or less moral than believers. There is no study anywhere that indicates atheists do bad things more often than believers. Moreover, if atheists were such horrible people, we'd expect the nonbeliever population to be disproportionately represented in prisons. No official government surveys are carried out in the United States of the religion of inmates, but informal surveys indicate nonbelievers are actually underrepresented in prisons.[3]

In any event, it's obvious that the belief that atheists are immoral is not based on relevant factual information. It is noteworthy that this prejudice took root long before open expression of disbelief in God was a common phenomenon. Until the nineteenth century, it was exceedingly rare for atheists to be open about their disbelief—with good reason, as a public declaration of atheism was sure to end in social death if not actual death. In fact, it's only been fairly recently that large numbers of people have voluntarily identified as atheists, agnostics, humanists, or just plain "not religious." So it's not as though people studied and compared the behavior of believers and nonbelievers and drew the conclusion that nonbelievers are a bad group of people. To the contrary, many believers have simply assumed that the conduct of atheists *must* be worse than the conduct of theists because in their minds God is closely, if vaguely, associated with morality.

This prejudice is a problem if we are going to live in religiously pluralistic societies, with a large component of nonbelievers. Religious animosities can provide fertile ground for social turmoil. The good news is some of this prejudice will gradually disappear as more people come into contact with nonbelievers. To some extent, prejudice toward nonbelievers is a function of the general lack of familiarity with open nonbelievers. Negative stereotypes concerning nonbelievers persist in part because people don't have personal experiences that contradict the stereotypes. If you are told for most of your life that atheists are immoral and untrustworthy and you never have the opportunity to know an atheist personally, there is a strong likelihood that a negative image of atheists will continue to guide your outlook. (This is one reason it's important for atheists to "come out of the closet.")

But apart from reducing animosity toward nonbelievers there is the separate issue of getting believers and nonbelievers talking to each other about issues of common concern. As I have already discussed, we should aim for a secular society in which everyone can debate policy issues, including issues that have moral implications, in terms that everyone can understand and evaluate. For this we need some shared understanding of morality. This is difficult to achieve if most people persist in thinking God—or, better said, *their* God—is the source for morality: that we need to rely on God's directives to tell right from wrong.

What I will address in this chapter is whether this association between God and morality can be justified. Must we rely on God's directives to provide us with a foundation for morality? Or is it the case that it is our own understanding of right and wrong that undergirds morality? Can God—does God—really tell us what to do?

Living Together: The Purpose of Morality

In considering difficult issues, it is often beneficial to clear one's mind of preconceptions. This is the method I would recommend we follow in thinking about morality. Morality is something that affects all of us, so whether or not anyone has given any thought to the foundations of morality, most people will come to this topic with various presumptions—presumptions that reflect their upbringing, education, background beliefs, and life experience. These will color any discussion of the topic. So to the extent possible, we should try to approach this topic afresh.

To begin, to make sure we are on the same page, let me indicate what I mean by morality. "Morality" refers to those standards of conduct we utilize to distinguish right from wrong and to encourage and discourage certain types of behavior. ("Ethics" is sometimes used as a synonym for morality, but it also has the special connotation of a study or analysis of morality.) These standards can be of different types—very general principles, such as "be kind to others," rules, such as "keep your promises," or specific directives, such as "don't hit your brother." I will refer to all these different standards as "norms."

So, if we are starting from the ground up, let's ask a basic question. Why should we have morality? What is its purpose? Note that I am not asking, "Why should *I* be moral?"—a question often posed in intro philosophy courses. I do not mean to be dismissive of this question—and I will touch upon it briefly later—but it raises a different set of issues than the ones we should concentrate on now. What I am interested in is reflection on the institution of morality as a whole. Why bother having morality?

One way to begin to answer this question is just to look at how morality functions, and has functioned, in human societies. What is it that morality allows us to do? What can we accomplish when (most) people behave morally that we would not be able to accomplish otherwise? Broadly speaking, morality appears to serve these related purposes: it creates stability, provides security, ameliorates harmful conditions, fosters trust, and facilitates cooperation in achieving shared and complementary goals. In other words, morality enables us to live together and, while doing so, improve the conditions under which we live.

This is not necessarily an exhaustive list of the functions of morality, nor do I claim to have explained the functions in the most accurate and precise way possible. But I am confident my list is a fair approximation of some of the key functions of morality.[4]

How do moral norms serve these functions? In following moral norms we engage in behavior that enables these functions of morality to be fulfilled. When we obey norms like "don't kill" and "don't steal," we help ensure the security and stability of society. It really doesn't take a genius to figure out why, but that hasn't stopped some geniuses from drawing our attention to the importance of moral norms. As the seventeenth century English philosopher Thomas Hobbes and many others have pointed out, if we always had to fear being injured or having our property stolen, we could never have any rest. Our lives would be "solitary, poor, nasty, brutish, and short."[5] Besides providing security and stability by prohibiting certain actions, moral norms also promote collaboration by encouraging certain actions and by providing the necessary framework for the critical practice of the "promise"—that is, a commitment that allows others to rely on me. Consider a simple example, one that could reflect circumstances in the Neolithic Era as much as today. I need a tool you have to complete a project, so I ask you to lend it to me. You hesitate to lend me the tool, but you also believe you are obliged to help me if such help doesn't significantly harm you. Moreover, I promise to return the tool. You lend me the tool; I keep my promise to return the tool. This exchange fosters trust between us. Both of us will be more inclined to cooperate with each other in the future. Our cooperation will likely improve our respective living conditions.

Multiply this example millions of times and you get a sense of the numerous transactions among people that allow a peaceful, stable, prospering society to emerge. You also can imagine how conditions would deteriorate if moral norms were not followed. Going back to my tool example, let us imagine you do not respond positively to my request for assistance. This causes resentment and also frustrates my ability to carry out a beneficial project. I am also less likely to assist you if you need help. Or say you do lend me a tool, but I keep it instead of returning it as promised. This causes distrust, and you are less likely to assist me (and others) in the future. Multiplied many times such failures to follow moral norms can result in mistrust, reduced cooperation, and even violence. If I do not return that tool peacefully, you may resort to brute force to reacquire it.

Fortunately, over time, humans have acted in ways that further the objectives of morality far more often than in ways that frustrate these objectives. Early humans were able to establish small communities that survived, in part, because most members of the community followed moral norms. These small communities eventually grew larger, again, in part because of moral norms. In this instance, what was critical was the extension of the scope or range of moral norms to those outside one's immediate community. Early human communities were often at war with each other. Tribe members acted benevolently only to fellow members of their tribe; outsiders were not regarded as entitled to the same treatment. One of the earliest moral revolutions was the extension of cooperative behavior—almost surely based initially on trade—to members of other communities, which allowed for peaceful interaction and the coalescing of small human groups into larger groups. This process has been repeated over the millennia of human existence (with frequent, sanguinary interruptions) until we have achieved something like a global moral community.

This outline of morality and its history is so simple, I am sure some will consider it simplistic. I have covered in a couple of paragraphs what others devote thick tomes to.[6] But it suffices for my purposes. The main points are that in considering morality we can see that it serves certain functions and these functions are related to human interests. Put another way, we can describe morality and its purposes without bringing God into the picture. So why bring him in? Why the oft-repeated claim that God is necessary for morality—that without God everything is permitted?

Is Morality Based on God's Commandments?

Many religious individuals claim that God is necessary to ground morality. Yes, we follow moral norms, but what is it that obliges us to follow moral norms? And how do we know which norms we should follow? Isn't there disagreement among humans about what's right and wrong, and if so, don't we need God to resolve these disputes? As Stephen Carter argued in *The Culture of Disbelief*, the idea of a moral authority "implies the existence of an arbiter," and the will of God seems to fit this description better than the will of some philosophers.[7]

Undeniably, the view that God is needed to provide a foundation for morality has had many adherents—until the last couple of centuries almost everyone apart from a few philosophers had this view—and among its adherents have been some very smart people, including respected jurists such as Antonin Scalia, so we need to take this position seriously.[8]

Because this is an important issue, we should strive to be precise. In saying that God's commands provide the basis for morality, we can mean several different, albeit related, things. First, we could be saying that we do not have a way to determine what is right or wrong apart from God's commands. God is not only connected to morality; his commands resolve definitively what we should do. Some action is right just *because* God commands us to do it (and wrong *because* God commands us not to do it). To talk of moral obligations apart from God's commands literally makes no sense. Second, we could be saying that although in some instances we can distinguish right from wrong without reference to God's commands, it is God's commands that imbue moral norms with the force of obligation. Moreover, God's commands supplement the moral norms we can discern through the use of our reason, and his directives resolve any moral disputes humans may have. Third, we could be saying that the institution of morality is no more than an arbitrary set of norms unless there is a deity who serves as the ultimate moral authority. This position is connected to the frequent claim that without God there is no "objective" right or wrong; moral norms are just expressions of personal preference. Fourth, we could be saying that moral norms lack the ability to motivate us if there is no God to reward and punish, whether in this life or a possible afterlife. As indicated, these positions are related, and there is some conceptual overlap, so to keep them distinct for the purpose of analysis, I suggest we label them. The first position is God as moral dictator; the second is God as moral adviser; the third is God as commissioner of morality; and the fourth is God as moral enforcer. For some believers, to the extent they consider the issue of God's relationship to morality, he plays all four roles. We will see, though, that God does not and cannot carry out the first two roles. With respect to the third and fourth roles, his services are not required.

God as Moral Dictator

Long ago, Plato, in his dialogue *Euthyphro*, exposed the fundamental flaw in the first role assigned to God, that is, God as moral dictator, a being whose word defines what is right and wrong.[9] Here is the dilemma that exposes the flaw. Either there is a way for us to determine what is right and wrong apart from God's commands or there isn't. Do you think torturing a child for amusement is morally wrong? How about killing someone to take over their property? Presumably, the answer is "yes," as it would be to any other question that asks about conduct anyone (or at least anyone who is not pathological) would consider morally repugnant. This indicates that we do have a sense of what is right and wrong independent of any commandment from God. You don't need to study the Bible to find out whether torturing a child is wrong. If we have this sense of right and wrong apart from God's commandments, then we do not have to rely on God's commandments. We can determine for ourselves what we should do.

Suppose, though, that a believer insists that nothing is morally obligatory or forbidden apart from God's commandments. Something is good only because God commands it. This implies we have no independent standard for what is morally right or wrong, good or bad. But if we have no such standard, how do we know that what God commands is the right thing to do? How do we know whether God himself is good and worthy of being obeyed? The answer is we do not know. God's commands are merely arbitrary edicts that we are incapable of evaluating. As with a dictator, we are just supposed to obey him, numbly and blindly. Furthermore, if God's commandments are to be followed without question, because there is no way we can tell right from wrong, then he could command us to do things that *seem* horrible—such as torturing a child—and, according to the dogmatic believer, we would obliged to obey.

One response sometimes made by believers at this juncture is that God would not command us to perform horrible actions because he is good, indeed perfectly good. Therefore, to imagine possible scenarios in which God orders to do a horrible thing is to engage in idle speculation. But this response fails because it assumes we can characterize God as morally good when, by hypothesis, we have no way of determining what is morally good. If we do not know what is good or bad, right or wrong, independently of God's commands, for all we know he is either malevolent or capricious.

And given some of the commandments attributed to God in the Bible or the Qur'an, there are ample grounds for regarding the deity as a malevolent spirit. The Old Testament is replete with divine directives that make God look like a homicidal maniac and an "ethnic cleanser" without equal. See, for example, Exod. 23: 23–30, 34: 11–16 and Deut. 20: 16–18 (God instructs Israelites to destroy Canaanites and various other inhabitants of the land Israelites are to possess); Num. 31: 17–18 (Moses angrily instructs his warriors to kill all male children among captives as well as women who "have known man" but to preserve virgins as sex slaves). Nowadays, of course, the tendency among most, but not all, believers is to pass over such passages in embarrassed silence or to interpret them in an allegorical fashion so that God doesn't come off as a murderer. This reaction is due to our contemporary sense of right and wrong, which doesn't permit us to conceive of God as a bloodthirsty monster who plays favorites and assists his chosen people while raining destruction on everyone else. This reaction also indicates that it is our moral sense that believers use to give content to God's supposed commandments; it's not the other way around.

To sum up: either God commands certain actions for a morally appropriate reason, in which case it's that reason that makes the action right, or God has no reasons for his commands. Either we are able to know what is right and wrong apart from God's commands, in which case there is no need for direction from God, or God's commands are arbitrary edicts and have no moral value. Either way God does not serve as the foundation for morality.

God as Moral Adviser

Let us proceed now to God as moral adviser. Believers may respond to the dilemma just posed by conceding that we do have a sense of right and wrong independent of God's commands. On this view, God has created us with the ability to arrive at the proper moral conclusion in some cases by use of our reason. Moral norms are knowable by humans. God still maintains a significant role in establishing moral norms, however. God has instituted morality by organizing the universe in such a way that there is moral goodness and moral norms that further this goodness. In addition, God speaks to us through revelation to supplement the moral truths that are discoverable by reason. These revelations add to the moral norms that we can discern through the use of reason and correct any misinterpretations humans may make of moral norms.

Many Christian theologians and philosophers have maintained a view similar to the above. In particular, those in the natural law tradition, such as Thomas Aquinas, have embraced something like this. The principal advantage of such a position for those who want to continue to use religion as a source of morality is that it keeps God involved in morality while at the same time recognizing that humans are able to make moral judgments on their own. Such a view appears to escape from the dilemma that dooms the position that God is the sole source of right and wrong, good and bad.

It does not work, though. Forget for the moment that those in the natural law tradition have had some sharp disagreements about what is "natural" and, therefore, moral. Two important points. First, insofar as this view admits that humans are able to make moral judgments on their own without the aid of divine commands, then God, once again, drops out of the picture. In conceding that human reason is capable of discerning moral truths, this position also concedes that God is, to that extent, irrelevant. (No, I'm not forgetting that God's endorsement of morality somehow ensures objectivity. I will reach that issue in the next chapter.)

Second point. To the extent God supposedly remains morally relevant on this view, it is through the obligatory nature of commands whose goodness we cannot discern through reason. Immediately then, we are faced with the same problem we could not solve when we discussed God's role as moral dictator. How do we know that these commands are morally valid? By hypothesis, we are not able to understand the reasons behind them. We are asked to accept these commands on trust—blind faith, if you will. One could argue that this trust is justified because of God's superior knowledge, but does this superior knowledge translate into superior moral understanding? Is this not the same line we are given by tyrants: trust me, follow me, I know better.

It cannot be denied that there have been alleged divine commands that seem strange, if not wholly inconsistent with accepted moral norms. We have discussed some already. Even Aquinas—without doubt the most important and influential Christian theologian—admitted as much. Aquinas felt compelled to discuss how it was possible that God had apparently commanded things that contradicted natural law, in particular his commandments to Abraham to kill his son (Gen. 22:2), to the Israelites to steal from the Egyptians (Exod. 12:35), and to Hosea to marry "a wife of harlotry" (Hosea 1:2). Aquinas's weak explanation is that whatever God commands cannot be an injustice, because whatever is done by God is, in some way, "natural."[10] Of course, this is just arguing in circles, so it is not really an explanation at all.

Even more bewilderingly, God appears to change his mind about what is morally obligatory or permissible. The Church of Jesus Christ of Latter-day Saints, also known as the Mormons, permitted polygamy early in its history based on a divine revelation. However, in 1890, the leader of the church, Wilford Woodruff, had another revelation that told him to instruct the Mormons to cease practicing polygamy. That this about-face was due solely to revelation, and not to moral reasoning, is evident from the heartfelt and anguished statement of President Woodruff in which he confessed it was only because God expressly commanded him that he told the Mormons to end plural marriages: "I should have let all the temples go out of our hands; I should have gone to prison myself, and let every other man go there, had not the God of heaven commanded me to do what I did do."[11]

There is no need to multiply examples. My purpose is not to catalogue the weird things God has supposedly commanded us to do, or the various second thoughts the deity appears to have had about his instructions. This is a short book. My point is that the position that sees God as providing advice that goes beyond what we humans can determine on our own does nothing to support the claim that God is indispensable to morality. Precisely because his commands are supposedly outside the sphere of our moral competence, we are not justified in saying that his commands represent morally valid norms. We are not capable of evaluating their moral character. It would be like asking a child to determine whether a page full of equations described the behavior of subatomic particles or was merely a string of numbers and symbols without meaning.

To sum up: this view of God as supplementing our moral knowledge with his commands does not, in the final analysis, preserve any significant moral role for God's commands.

The Revelation Problem—Why We Cannot Know God's Commands

There is a larger problem that undermines God's role either as a moral dictator or moral adviser. It's an epistemological problem that's not fully appreciated by many believers. It's not possible to have a divine command theory of morality unless there is some way one can establish that God has communicated his directives to us. *The problem is we cannot know when God has spoken.* Consequently, we cannot know the contents of God's commands because we cannot know whether he has issued any commands.

How are God's commands supposedly transmitted to us? Through revelation, which is usually understood as a communication from God, or some other supernatural entity such as an angel, in which some significant truth is revealed to an individual. These truths can be statements about a number of things, such as God's nature, God's relationship to humans, predictions of things to come, or commands, some of which have moral implications. The three major monotheistic religions, Judaism, Christianity, and Islam, and many other religions, such as Mormonism, are based largely on revelations allegedly made to various prophetic figures. It is no exaggeration to say that the critical core of most religious beliefs is constituted by revelation. The vast majority of these revelations are set forth in texts that are regarded as the sacred, governing texts of the religion. Sacred scriptures function as the record of divine self-disclosure. As the Catechism of the Catholic Church states, "Sacred Scripture is the speech of God as it is put down in writing under the breath of the Holy Spirit."[12] Religions differ over what texts are sacred; indeed, what principally distinguishes one religion from another are disagreements over which revelations are authentic.

Authenticity. That's a problem isn't it? What makes one alleged revelation a divine or divinely inspired message and the other the ravings of a madman, the mutterings of a self-deluded enthusiast, or the invention of a con man? A revelation is something that by definition is not transmitted to humans in the standard way we acquire information. Also, the content of the revelation is typically something that exceeds our powers of perception. As the Catholic Church has explained in its official statement on revelation, through revelation God has chosen to share with humans "those divine treasures that totally transcend the understanding of the human mind."[13] God's sharing can be done via some inner nonverbal experience, an inner verbal experience, a sign, or a vision, that is, we can feel God's presence, we can "hear" God inside our head, we can interpret an apparent natural occurrence as a supernatural manifestation, or we can see and/or hear God (or, more likely, one of his agents, as, at least for the Abrahamic religions, God hasn't appeared much since biblical times). These are general categories; theologians can subdivide them further. Whatever the mode of sharing, the distinguishing feature of a revelation is that it involves a privileged access to the divine such that the claim that a revelation occurred cannot be verified or disconfirmed in the standard way reports of ordinary events are verified or disconfirmed. You say it's raining outside. The truth of that assertion is settled easily enough. You say that yesterday you were hit on the head by a baseball. This may require a bit more work, but, again, information that's accessible to anyone who is interested in the question can in principle be obtained to confirm or refute your claim. But we cannot confirm or refute transcendental experiences. The person who's experienced the revelation may be absolutely certain it occurred, but her subjective experience is inaccessible to others.

This problem has long been recognized. Thomas Hobbes discussed the impossibility of confirming that another person has had a revelation:

> When God speaketh to man, it must be either immediately; or by mediation of another man, to whom he had formerly spoken by himself immediately. How God speaketh to a man immediately, may be understood by those well enough, to whom he hath so spoken; but how the same should be understood by another, is hard, if not impossible to know. For if a man pretend to me, that God hath spoken to him supernaturally, and immediately, and I make doubt of it, I cannot easily perceive what argument he can produce, to oblige me to believe it. ...
>
> To say he hath spoken to him in a Dream, is no more than to say he dreamed that God spake to him; which is not of force to win belief from any man ...[14]

In other words, for those not experiencing the revelation, skepticism is the rational response. The more plausible explanation for a revelation will *always* be some natural cause as opposed to a supernatural cause. There is no good reason for me to conclude that God actually spoke to you. Instead, it is much more probable that you had a dream, you are interpreting ordinary thoughts as divine communications because of your religious enthusiasm, or you had a psychological disturbance. (You could also be lying, but for our purposes, let's assume sincerity.)

Mormons are sometimes ridiculed because Joseph Smith, the founding prophet for that faith, is the only one who had the ability to translate the Book of Mormon from so-called reformed Egyptian into English, which he accomplished by using a seer stone placed in the bottom of a large hat. The seer stone acted as the instrument for God's revelation. The hat was drawn tightly around Smith's face so no one else could view the stone and the letters it supposedly revealed. Such a scene fairly calls out for mockery. Those skeptically inclined likely regard Smith's actions as the conduct of a con man or a person woefully self-deluded. However, much the same could be said for any supposed prophet's revelation. There's always a good reason to doubt the report of a revelation.

The New Testament indicates that, from the earliest days, there were plenty of scoffers around. From the author of 2 Peter we learn that there were many who considered the stories about Jesus "cleverly devised myths" (2 Peter 1:16–18). In rebuttal, the author essentially pleads, "Hey, I and some others actually heard God say, 'This is my beloved son, with whom I am well pleased.' Really we did. Can't help it if you weren't there." But those who were not there have good reason to be suspicious about a report from some unlearned fisherman that he heard God speak from the heavens.

Similarly, the angel Gabriel first appeared to Muhammad in a dream, after Muhammad had withdrawn to a secluded cave for mediation and prayer.[15] Skepticism about the revelations Muhammad received seems amply justified. To paraphrase Hobbes, Muhammad's report that Gabriel spoke to him in a dream is no different than Muhammad saying he dreamt that Gabriel spoke to him. A reasonable person should be reluctant to accept revelations, whether they emanate from a person talking into a hat or a person talking about his dreams.

This is not to say that people cannot be persuaded to accept a claim that someone else has experienced a revelation. No, obviously, there are billions of people who *have* accepted such claims. That's how we have the religions we do. Paul found followers; Muhammad found followers; Joseph Smith found followers. Not everyone is capable of critical thinking, especially when those around them believe there has been a revelation. In a crowd of believers, it's difficult not to believe. If one inhabits a world where supernatural spirits are presumed abundant, and one's understanding of human psychology is poor—in other words, if one inhabits the world prior to the twentieth century—then one will be susceptible to the claim that God has spoken to some prophet. The point here is not about whether revelations are ever believed; instead it is about whether there is a rational justification for believing them. If we do evaluate a claim of revelation rationally, there will always be more grounds for rejecting it than accepting it.

The problem with revelation goes deeper, however. Even the person experiencing the purported revelation cannot plausibly claim to know it is God who is showing himself through the experience. Yes, the person has a subjective sense of certainty about the revelation, but what does that establish? Such a feeling or sensation cannot logically be interpreted as a revealing of the divine unless the person has had some *prior* experience of the divine to which the current experience can be compared. And, of course, any prior experience would have to be verified in the same manner. So even the person undergoing the mystical experience cannot know that it really is God conveying a message; it could be the devil, a sensation the person himself has unconsciously generated, or the imaginative interpretation of an ordinary thought.

Bringing in the devil as an alternative hypothesis is not an outlandish move, by the way. If we are going to entertain the possibility of supernatural beings, there's no reason there can't be demons. In addition, no less an authority than that esteemed theologian Augustine specifically warned believers that demons can easily impersonate angels. In fact, according to Augustine, believers cannot distinguish demons from angels without God's mercy.[16] But how is one to know whether God's mercy has been activated? Augustine provides no answer.

Some may think that visions, that is, apparitions that seem to appear outside the mind of the believer, provide some solid evidence of a manifestation of the divine, at least to the believer himself. Not really. Leaving aside the obvious explanation of hallucination, there is again the problem of connecting the experience to God. We say where there's smoke, there's fire, but that is because we have experience of smoke being correlated with fire. Contrast the smoke/fire situation with a vision of a figure that suddenly appears before me announcing it's an angel of the Lord. What experience do I have of correlations between visions such as this and God? None. God is transcendent; he is outside the natural world, so, by hypothesis, I cannot experience God directly. Therefore, I have no more warrant for inferring this vision is a revelation from God than I do for inferring that it is an attempt at deceit by the devil, an alien being, a trick produced by some natural process, or a projection from my subconscious.

But what about visions that appear simultaneously to a number of people? Aren't these credible manifestations of the divine, or at least something outside the natural order? Sacred texts do discuss some such alleged mass visions, for example, the story of the descent of the Holy Spirit at Pentecost during which the third person of the Trinity appears to the apostles in the guise of "tongues as of fire" (Acts 2:1–4). Doesn't this intersubjective experience have some credibility?

Again, we need to distinguish what is rational for someone not experiencing the vision to believe and the psychological state of the persons undergoing the experience. For those of us living today, one weighty reason not to credit the Pentecost story is that we don't have access to this event except through the much-edited, much-copied-over writings of an individual (or individuals) who lived about 1,900 years ago and who was a member of the cult that had grown up around Jesus of Nazareth. Furthermore, Luke, to whom this part of Acts is usually attributed, did not even witness the Pentecost event himself. This is just to scratch the surface of our reasons for skepticism. For example, we are also aware today that the contents of the New Testament were the subject of much controversy in the first four centuries of the Common

Era, and there were many stories about Jesus and his followers that did not make the final cut.

In addition, in assessing claims of visions of God or his agents that allegedly appear to a number of people simultaneously, we must consider the preexisting beliefs of the persons claiming to experience the vision. If the Pentecost vision had announced to the apostles, "Hey, you've got this Jesus thing all wrong—everything will be explained to you in about 1,900 years by a prophet named L. Ron Hubbard," that would be noteworthy because it would suggest the vision was not some imagined projection based on preexisting beliefs. As it is, this purported vision is all too similar to alleged mass sightings of other supernatural beings through the ages—*they almost always reflect the beliefs of the people experiencing the vision.* For example, not many Jews have visions of the Virgin Mary. Pagan Greeks and Romans had mass sightings of their gods, but not the angel Gabriel. Why don't we believe them? If we have no reason to credit the mass sightings of Dionysius, Demeter, and all the other pagan deities that occurred in the era before Christianity, we have no reason to credit the mass sightings of Jesus, the Virgin Mary, or other supernatural beings with a Christian brand that have occurred in the Christian era.[17] People project the beliefs they already hold, which is why today in Christian countries it's always Mary or Jesus appearing on grilled cheese sandwiches, not Aphrodite or Apollo.

Admittedly, those who are experiencing the mass vision themselves have *some* reason for thinking they are all experiencing *something*, as they have intersubjective verification. But they have no warrant for going beyond that limited claim. We are familiar with cause and effect in the natural world. We do not have familiarity with the realm of the supernatural. Even if I am experiencing some sort of vision along with several others, it would not be rational for me to conclude this vision is a manifestation of God or one of his agents. I do not possess the prior experience of God that would justify this claim.

There is no escaping this conclusion: revelations are neither confirmable nor self-authenticating. To believe in a revelation requires an act of faith, as the Catholic Church candidly admits.[18] As the late Pope John Paul II remarked of the revelation that Jesus is the son of God, "one can only accept it or reject it."[19] In other words, one cannot gather evidence and argue for its truth. There is no evidential basis for believing in revelations, and, therefore, someone who has not made a prior faith commitment—which itself is an act without rational support—cannot be expected to believe them.

Let's take stock for a moment. We entered into this discussion of revelation because it is through revelation that we are supposedly made aware of God's commands. If God is to have any direct role to play with respect to morality, either as moral dictator or moral adviser, we would need to be able to receive instructions from him. Our analysis of revelation has established that God effectively has no way to communicate his commands to us. Even if he were to transmit a command through a prophet, we would have no way of confirming this was a divine command. But the situation is even worse than this. What purported revelations we do have from God are inconsistent.

The various religions that base their creeds on revelation rely on differing and contradictory revelations. Even within Judaism, Christianity, or Islam, there are deep disagreements about how an alleged revelation is to be interpreted. Orthodox Jews disagree with Reform and Conservative Jews, Protestants disagree with Catholics, Sunni with Shiite, and there are dissenters within Mormonism who still practice polygamy. Given these disputes over revelation among believers, revelation becomes useless as a means of grasping God's commands. One God prohibits drinking alcohol, while another God says it is permissible; one God demands male circumcision, while another God says you can hold on to your foreskin; one God prohibits divorce, while another God is fine with that; one God prohibits contraception, while another God has no objection; one God prohibits the consumption of shellfish, while another God says *bon appetit*; one God prohibits work on Saturday, another on Sunday, and yet another has no objection to work on any day. Of course, the sharpest conflicts arise when one God tells his followers to stand firm against, and if necessary to fight, the followers of another God—a situation that still arises in the twenty-first century. The day I was writing this passage, I saw in the newspaper a reference to a 2010 speech by Mahmoud Abbas, president of the Palestinian Authority, in which he stated that "Jerusalem and its environs are a trust that Allah entrusted to us. Saving it from the settlement monster and the danger of Judaization ... is a personal commandment incumbent on all of us."[20] Presumably, the Jewish inhabitants of Israel do not believe this particular commandment is incumbent upon *them*, especially as their God tells them to remain in Jerusalem.

Monotheism is often held up as some great intellectual or moral advance over the polytheism that prevailed among the ancient Romans and Greeks. With respect to the utility of commands from God, nothing has really changed. Instead of disputes among the Olympian gods, we now have disputes among the various versions of the Jewish God, the Christian God, the Islamic God, the Mormon God, and so forth. I referenced earlier Plato's dialogue *Euthyphro* in which he pointed out the flaws in the view that we have no understanding of morality apart from divine commands. In one passage in the dialogue, the character Socrates illustrates one of the problems with this view, using a polytheistic example:

> [I]t seems that what is pleasing to the gods is also hateful to them. Thus, Euthyphro, it would not seem strange at all if what you are now doing in punishing your father were pleasing to Zeus, but hateful to Cronus and Uranus, and welcome to Hephaestus, but odious to Hera, and if any of the other gods disagree about the matter, satisfactory to some of them, and odious to others.[21]

Substitute "Jewish God" for "Zeus," "Christian God" for "Cronus," and all the various versions of our contemporary God for the pagan gods and we can make a very similar assertion. What is satisfactory to one religion's God is odious to another religion's God.

There is no rational decision process that would enable humans to determine on the basis of accessible evidence which of the various competing revelations available to us is really *the* authentic revelation of God. Faith, not reason, is the basis for accepting any revelation, and one cannot say one faith is more reasonable than another as any faith commitment is undertaken in the absence of reason.

God cannot tell us what to do because, among other reasons, we are not able to recognize a command from God. Because God cannot effectively communicate with us, we cannot base morality on his commands.

The Relevance of God's Commands for Public Policy

To recapitulate, in a secular state we cannot have religious doctrines determine public policy. Otherworldly concerns are not the business of the state. Moreover, in a secular society we should not have believers interject their religious beliefs into policy discussions. This prevents any meaningful dialogue. To the objection that religious views have an important function in those public policy debates that raise moral concerns, the appropriate response is that religious doctrines do not provide a basis for presenting moral concerns. Religious doctrines are derived from revelation, and there is no rational way to confirm a revelation or to prefer one revelation over another. Moral concerns can and must be framed in secular terms.

The notion that moral norms are derived from God's commands is a myth; at times it is a pernicious myth. One understandable reason why this myth has had such a tenacious hold on people is that religious institutions have played a large role in inculcating and reinforcing moral norms. Many children first learn to memorize basic moral norms in a religious setting, and clergy have been looked upon as moral authorities. However, as our analysis has shown, divine commands do not and cannot determine the content of our moral norms. We are the ones who determine the content of these moral norms. This has always been true. It's true for devout believers, even if they don't acknowledge it. They selectively pick among the many competing commands attributed to God, and once their selection is made, they interpret them in the way they think best. In other words, they use their moral sense to determine what norms they find acceptable and only those acceptable norms receive the honorary designation of a divine command.

Sacred texts are malleable, as we have seen. There are many believers who either ignore or creatively interpret passages that appear to command acts uncongenial to their contemporary sensibilities. Does Leviticus 20:13 condemn gays to death? ("If a man lies with a male as with a woman, both of them have committed an abomination; they shall be put to death.") Well, Jesus did away with the old law, and "there is neither Jew nor Greek, there is neither slave nor free, there is neither male nor female; for you are all in Christ Jesus" (Gal. 3:28). You can spin sacred scriptures any way you want. Who's to say you're wrong?

Use of religious texts and doctrines in discussing moral issues is not only ultimately pointless; it also impedes understanding and creates obstacles to meaningful discussion. One problem with those who claim to find morality in God's commands is that when they cloak their reasoning in religious garb, they obscure the basis for their reasoning and often fail to consider the factors relevant to a moral judgment. Instead of focusing on factors that may be relevant to an issue, too many believers spend their time leafing through their Bible or Qur'an—or, even worse, seeking the advice of some religious leader—trying to find the appropriate words of wisdom. Not only does such a practice tend to make our moral judgments ill-informed, but it also leads to unnecessary antagonism and impasse. The scriptures are malleable, but conclusions, once reached, tend not to be very flexible—how can one negotiate over God's word? People with differing scriptures and differing interpretations of the same scripture face off, screaming at each other across picket lines, with perhaps the only thing uniting them being their distrust of atheists.

Above I cited dueling scriptures that relate to attitudes we should have toward gays. A hotly contested public policy issue at the moment is the issue of legalization of same-sex marriage. This is an issue with moral implications. Should we turn to the scriptures for guidance? I hope by this point in the book, the reader will respond, "No." Instead we should look at the underlying objectives of an institution such as marriage, expressly articulate and consider our background moral principles, and examine relevant data to determine whether legalization of same-sex marriage would further the objectives of the institution of marriage and be consistent with our moral principles. This type of discussion can engage everyone; it need not have, it should not have, any reference to supposed divine directives. We should talk to each other, not hide behind alleged commands from God.

Those to Whom God Does Speak

Although I have provided reasons why even those who think they have received a revelation should be skeptical that they actually have been in communication with God, I am realist enough to recognize that many believers will continue to think they receive communications from God despite what I say. One reason I am confident in this conclusion is that I was a believer myself. When I was a believer, I was convinced God did communicate with me. Certain thoughts in my head I interpreted as God talking with me. I'm doubtful any argument would have persuaded me otherwise. The experience was too immediate, too vivid, too encompassing.

Talking with God is an everyday experience for many believers. Presumably they too have the same strong sense of an external presence as I had. To the extent I discuss this issue with friends or relatives who are religious, they confirm this. Studies of religious believers also confirm their certitude about being in communication with God.[22] So why shouldn't those who speak with God on a regular basis accept that the prophets of their respective religions had revelations?

I could carry my argument one step further by asking believers why it is their respective religions do not permit them to have a public revelation, instead confining them to a private revelation. In other words, most religions maintain that revelations that inform us about general, important matters concerning the relations between God and his creation either stopped at a certain point in time or are channeled only through specific individuals. For Jews, there is no public revelation after the Tanakh; for Christians, none after the New Testament; for Muslims, Muhammad had the definitive word. Mormons do accept continuous revelation, but only through the president of their church, who is also considered a prophet. God can inform ordinary, contemporary believers that someone is sick or pregnant or that a car will be repaired on time (a private revelation I had at seventeen), but any revelation that challenges accepted doctrine is peremptorily ruled inauthentic. Isn't that strange? Doesn't this suggest that the whole notion of basing important beliefs on revelation is questionable? There is nothing but an arbitrary line that separates the "truths" Gabriel reveals to me in a dream from the "truths" Gabriel revealed to Muhammad in a dream. Why are Muhammad's dreams entitled to more deference than my dreams? Because he and his followers were successful in putting together an army?

But I will not pursue that line of thought. Among other reasons, this is not a missionary tract. My primary purpose is not to persuade people to stop believing in God. Instead, I want believers to recognize that if they hope to engage in policy discussions those who don't share their faith, they need to speak in terms everyone can understand. Even if you think God is talking to you and could tell *you* what to do, you need to recognize he can't tell *us* what to do.

* * * *

The arguments in this chapter have shown why God can't tell us what to do. Arguably, this is sufficient to establish that we need to thoroughly secularize our democratic discourse and keep religion out of public policy debates. If God can't tell us what to do, the believer who wants to interject her religious beliefs into a policy discussion really has nothing substantive to offer. But I don't expect all believers to be convinced at this stage because it's one thing to show that, logically, divine commands have no role to play in policy discussions that implicate morality and another to show that we can discuss morality without bringing religion into the discussion at all. Maybe God-talk in the context of morality cannot consist of more than rhetorical reminders that God stands behind the institution of morality, but perhaps that rhetoric serves some purpose. We still have that hobgoblin of moral subjectivity to worry about. Don't we need God to ensure we have objective moral values? In other words, don't we need God as the commissioner of morality? The next chapter will show why we do not require God's services in this regard.

Five

THE COMMON MORALITY
AND THE OBJECTIVITY THAT MATTERS

Without God, Isn't Morality Just Subjective?

Most of my professional life was spent as a practicing attorney. This occupation taught me many things, including the importance of the wording of questions. How a question is framed can shape expectations and answers.

Dear reader, I will give you a tip about cross-examination that by itself is worth the price of this book. (May you never have to experience cross-examination, but if you do, at least you will be prepared.) The lawyer who is cross-examining you is not asking for information—at least not if she is doing her job. Instead, she is trying to use your mouth to tell her client's version of events. In doing so, she will frame her questions aggressively. Her questions will contain implicit assumptions helpful to her client's case and will characterize facts in a way that assists her client's case. Here's a tip: in answering her questions, you do not have to accept the phrasing of the questions or the assumptions contained therein. "That's not how I would describe it" is a perfectly acceptable answer.

"If there is no God, then morality must be subjective, correct?" This is a favorite question of those who want to defend the importance

100

of religion for morality. Hidden in that question are a couple of assumptions. One assumption is God makes morality objective. We have already cast doubt on that proposition. Another assumption, all too often overlooked, is that morality must be either objective or subjective. We should not buy into that assumption. Morality is neither objective nor subjective as those terms are commonly understood. The term "objective" is typically used to designate statements that make assertions about some reality that exists independently of human desires, feelings, wishes. "Subjective" is used to designate statements that refer to our inner sentiments, that is, an individual's desires, feelings, wishes. But morality is not a description of a state of affairs. We don't acquire moral understanding merely by discovering a set of facts, whether it's facts about ourselves or facts about the world. Morality isn't constituted by a set of facts, but rather it is a set of human practices. These practices enable us to live together by, among other things, reducing social conflict.

In this section of the chapter, I will show that morality is not objective in the same way that statements of empirically verifiable facts are objective. This should not trouble us, however. When people worry about morality not being objective, they're concerned that morality may merely be a question of what feels right for any given individual, that there is no basis for saying someone else is wrong in their moral judgments. To quote Shakespeare, "there is nothing either good or bad, but thinking makes it so."[1] But even though moral judgments are not statements of objective facts, morality is still objective in the ways that matter: moral judgments are not arbitrary, we can have genuine disagreements about moral issues, people can be mistaken in their moral beliefs, and facts about the world are relevant to and inform our moral judgments. In other words, morality is not "subjective" as that term is usually interpreted. Moral judgments are not equivalent to scientific statements about the world, but neither are they merely expressions of personal preferences.

Let's start by looking at the function of moral judgments. The objective/subjective dichotomy implicitly assumes that moral judgments are used primarily to describe, so they must have either an objective or subjective reference. To the contrary, moral judgments have various practical applications; they are not used primarily as descriptive statements.

Consider these two statements:

Sam is hitting Chris in the face.

Without provocation, we ought not to hit people in the face.

Do these statements have identical functions? I suggest they do not. The first statement is used to convey factual information; it tells us about something that is happening. The second statement is in the form of a moral norm that reflects a moral judgment. Depending on the circumstances, the second statement can be used to instruct someone, condemn someone, admonish someone, exhort someone, confirm that the speaker endorses this norm, and so forth. The second statement has primarily practical, not descriptive, functions. Admittedly, in some circumstances, moral norms or descriptive counterparts of moral norms also can be used to make an assertion about the world, but they do not primarily serve to convey factual information.

The different functions of descriptive statements and moral norms were recognized and summarized nicely by the eighteenth-century Scottish philosopher David Hume, who remarked that from a statement about how things are—an "is" statement—we cannot infer a moral norm about how things should be—an "ought" statement.[2] Note that Hume did not say that facts are not relevant to moral judgments. Nor did he claim that our moral norms are subjective—although this is a position often mistakenly attributed to him. Instead, he maintained that a factual statement, considered in isolation, cannot imply a moral norm. An "is" statement and an "ought" statement are distinct classes of statement with distinct functions. Most people do not notice this difference in functions, at least not until it is drawn to their attention.

Because most of us have had moral norms inculcated into us, and our biology has been shaped by evolution to predispose us to certain reactions, our brains move effortlessly and immediately from an observation that Sam has hit Chris without provocation to the judgment that what Sam did was wrong. As a result, the functional and logical differences between factual statements and moral judgments are obscured, which leads some to think that moral judgments are determined to be true in the same way factual statements are determined to be true. Regarding moral judgments as descriptions of facts represents a misunderstanding of morality; it's a picture of morality that we need to discard.

In rejecting the proposition that moral judgments are equivalent to factual statements about the world—statements about coats, cats, or cars—I am not endorsing, nor did Hume endorse, the proposition that moral judgments are subjective. A subjective statement is still a descriptive statement that is determined to be true by reference to facts. It's simply a descriptive statement referring to facts about our inner states as opposed to something in the world. To claim that moral judgments are subjective is to claim that they are true or false based on how a particular person feels. That's not how we regard moral judgments, at least not outside the undergraduate philosophy seminar.

Again, Hume was perceptive on this point. He expressly denied that our moral judgments refer to our individual, subjective sentiments—which is why it is strange to see him labeled a subjectivist—explaining instead that they appeal to shared moral norms:

> When a man denominates another his enemy, his rival, his antagonist, his adversary, he is understood to speak the language of self-love, and to express sentiments peculiar to himself. . . . But when he bestows on any man the epithets of vicious or odious or depraved, he then speaks another language, and expresses sentiments in which, he expects, all his audience are to concur with him. He must here therefore depart from his private and particular situation, and must choose a point of view common to him with others.[3]

Our moral reasoning makes use of the "point of view common ... with others," not our private feelings.

And what is this point of view we share in common with others? It's what many ethicists refer to as the common morality. The common morality is composed of those core moral norms that have been accepted across cultures. For humans to live together in peace and prosper, we need to follow norms such as do not kill, do not steal, do not inflict pain gratuitously, tell the truth, keep your commitments, reciprocate acts of kindness, and so forth. The number of core norms is small, but they govern most of the transactions we have with other humans. This is why we see these norms in all functioning human societies, past and present. "[I]njunctions against violence, deceit, and betrayal . . . are familiar in every society and every legal system. They have been voiced in works as different as the Egyptian Book of the Dead, the Icelandic Edda, and the Bhagavad-Gita."[4] Any community in which these norms were lacking could not survive for long. We cannot live together in peace without these core moral norms. This shared core of moral norms represents the common heritage of civilized human society.

These shared norms also reflect the functions of morality as applied to the human condition. Earlier I observed that morality has certain functions, that is, it serves human interests and needs by creating stability, providing security, ameliorating harmful conditions, fostering trust, and facilitating cooperating in achieving shared and complementary goals. One can quibble about my wording, but that morality has something like these functions is beyond dispute. The norms of the common morality help ensure these functions are fulfilled by prohibiting killing, stealing, lying, and so forth. Given that humans are vulnerable to harm, that we depend upon the honesty and cooperation of others, that we are animals with certain physical and social needs, the norms of the common morality are indispensable.

We can see now how morality has the type of objectivity that matters. If we regard morality as a set of practices that has something like the functions I described, then not just any norm is acceptable as a moral norm. "Lie to others and betray them" is not going to serve the functions of morality. Because of our common human condition, morality is not arbitrary, nor is it subjective in any pernicious sense. When people express fears about morality being subjective, they are concerned about the view that what's morally permissible is simply what each person feels is morally permissible. But morality is not an expression of personal taste. Our common needs and interests place constraints on the content of morality. Similarly, if we regard morality as serving certain functions, we can see how facts about the world can inform our moral judgments. If morality serves to provide security and foster cooperation, then unprovoked assaults on others run counter to morality's aims. Indeed, these are among the types of actions that norms of the common morality try to prevent. For this reason when we are informed that Sam did hit Chris in the face without provocation, we quickly conclude that what Sam did was wrong, and his conduct should be condemned.

Facts by themselves do not entail moral judgments, but if we look upon morality as a set of practices that provide solutions to certain problems, for example, violence among members of the community, then we can see how facts are relevant to moral judgments. Part of the solution to violence among members of the community is to condemn violent acts and encourage peaceful resolution of disputes. Facts provide us with relevant information about how to best bring about this solution in particular circumstances.

Similarly, with a proper understanding of morality, we can also see how we can justify making inferences from factual statements to evaluative judgments. Recall that the fact/value gap prevents us from inferring a moral judgment from isolated statements of fact. But if we recognize and accept that morality serves certain functions and that the norms of the common morality help carry out these functions, the inference from facts to moral judgments is appropriate because we are not proceeding *solely* from isolated facts to moral judgments; instead, we are implicitly referencing the background institution of morality. An isolated factual observation cannot justify a moral judgment, but a factual observation embedded in a set of moral norms can justify a moral judgment.

At this point, two objections might be made to my characterization of morality and to my rejection of the objective/subjective distinction as it is commonly understood. First, assuming that the functions of morality I have described correspond to functions currently served by morality, this does not address the question of what the functions of morality *should* be. Haven't I just moved the fact/value gap back one step, from the level of an individual factual statement to the level of a description of the institution of morality as a whole? Put another way, explaining how morality functions doesn't address the issue of how it should function.

Second, even if morality should have the functions I have described, I have not explained why anyone should regard themselves obliged to follow moral norms. What is the origin of moral obligation? Isn't this where we need some objective standard, something completely independent of human interests to impose obligations?

Let's tackle the first objection. To begin, we should make a distinction between morality's functions and objectives. In chapter 4, I did not draw a sharp contrast between morality's functions and objectives because it was not necessary for the points I was making there. But in this context, where we want to make sure we are not making an illicit move from fact to value, we need to distinguish between a discussion of morality's functions, which involves factual claims, and a discussion of morality's objectives, which involves normative claims. One might concede that morality has the functions I have described, but still argue it should serve different objectives.

Interestingly, morality existed long before there was consideration of what its objectives should be. Just as morality did not originate with a set of divine commandments, neither did it originate with a set of well-reasoned commands from some human lawgiver. No person or set of persons designed moral institutions from scratch and proclaimed, "From now on, and for these reasons, this is how we all should behave." Before explicit moral norms, there was conduct modified by the reactions of others. Conduct disruptive to the community produced negative reactions; altruistic conduct produced positive reactions. In other words, patterns of behavior evolved before there was any explicit normative guidance. Even with the appearance of explicit normative guidance, in the form of orally communicated directives and rules, there was not necessarily any self-conscious reflection on these norms and consideration of whether morality should serve any purpose. Humans lived together for a long time before someone first asked, "Is this how we should be behaving?"

Of course, all that being said, we are at a stage in our cultural evolution where we can reflect on our moral norms and can discuss what objectives morality should have. So then the issue becomes: should morality have objectives that reflect the functions of morality that I have described, that is, serving human interests and needs by creating stability, providing security, ameliorating harmful conditions, fostering trust, and facilitating cooperating in achieving shared and complementary goals? Perhaps the best way to answer this question is with another question: what's the alternative? If morality should not aim to create stability, provide security, ameliorate harmful conditions, and so forth, what's the point of morality otherwise? To increase the production of cheese? One could maintain that cheese production is an overriding imperative and one could label this a moral imperative, but the reality is that for humans to live and work together we would still need something to fulfill the functions of what we now characterize as morality.

Perhaps we'd call it shmorality, but we'd still have similar norms and practices whatever its name.

Granted, some philosophers have argued that morality should have objectives somewhat different than the ones I have outlined. Various philosophers have argued that morality should aim at maximizing happiness, or producing a greater balance of pleasure over pain, or producing virtuous characters. Without digressing into a long discussion of ethical theory, I believe these views grasp certain aspects of the moral enterprise, but they mistakenly elevate part of what we accomplish through morality into the whole of it. There is no single simple principle that governs morality. Yes, we want to encourage people to be virtuous, that is, to be kind, courageous, and trustworthy, but to what end? Likewise, we want people to be happy, but exactly how do we measure units of happiness and how do we balance the happiness of different individuals against one another or against the happiness of the community? If we look at morality as a practical enterprise, something like the objectives I have outlined represent a better description of what we want morality to accomplish. (I say "something like" because I am not claiming to give the best possible description of morality's objectives.)

There is one important way in which someone could accept that morality serves functions similar to what I have described yet have a significantly different understanding of the objectives of morality, and that is by having a different understanding of the scope of morality. Although I have not expressly addressed this issue, I have implied that our moral norms apply to the whole human community. As I observed in the prior chapter, that's not the way it's always been nor, as a matter of logic, need it be that way. Early in human history, our moral obligations extended only to those in our tribe or clan, in part because the necessary conditions for cooperation between different tribes were absent. The notion of universal human rights is a fairly recent phenomenon. (I'll say more about this development in the next section.) One could maintain, without logical contradiction, that our moral obligations extend only to certain groups, be it one's relatives, one's co-religionists, one's proletarian comrades, those of "Aryan" blood, the Nietzschean elite, or so on. As a practical matter, however, it would be difficult to maintain such a moral view, certainly as a public morality. Those not in the Nietzschean elite are not going to cooperate with those who regard them as unworthy of moral concern, so in today's world of global interaction, the alternative to a moral community that encompasses all humans would be a world in which violence and force determines outcomes. Thus, in today's world, narrowing the scope of morality to exclude some groups of humans is more a matter of philosophical speculation than a realistic alternative. In-group tribal thinking that characterizes "outsiders" as lacking moral rights does still raise its hideous head from time to time—witness the Rwandan genocide—but it's difficult to sustain a functioning society on that basis.

The appropriate scope of morality is an interesting issue for those philosophically inclined, and much more could be said about it.[5] However, my limited purpose here is to show that we can have a naturalistic understanding of morality and its objectives that is widely shared and that provides a basis for factually informed discussion and reasoning about the moral issues that confront us. I think I've done that.

Let's turn now to the obligatory force of moral norms. Why "must" we follow the norms of the common morality, that is, how are these norms binding on us? There are two types of answer we can give here. Both are important so we need to keep them distinct. One answer would appeal to human psychology. The combination of our evolutionary inheritance and the moral training most of us receive dispose us to act morally.[6] We should not lose sight of this fact because if we were not receptive to moral norms, no reference to a divine command, no appeal to an ethical argument, could ever move us to behave morally. For a moral norm to act as a motivating reason to do, or refrain from doing, something, we must be the type of person who can respond to moral norms. Ethicists as far back as Aristotle have recognized this.[7] Good moral conduct owes much to moral training, and the most sublime exposition of the magnificence of the moral law will not persuade those who have been habituated into antisocial behavior. The sense of moral obligation, that tug that we feel toward doing the right thing, is explained, in part, by human psychology.

But in addition to a casual explanation of why we feel a sense of moral obligation, we also want an explanation of the reason for acknowledging moral obligations. In my view, it's largely a matter of logical consistency. *If* we accept the institution of morality, then we are tacitly agreeing to be bound by moral norms. We cannot logically maintain that moral norms apply to everyone except us. If we think it is morally wrong for others to break their promises to us, as a matter of logic we cannot say we are under no obligation to keep our promises. In saying an action is morally wrong, we are committed to making the same judgment regardless of whether it is I or someone else doing the action. In accepting the institution of morality, we are also accepting the obligations that come with this institution. Hence, there is a reason, not just a psychological cause, for acknowledging our obligation to follow moral norms.

Of course, even those who accept the institution of morality may fail to abide by moral norms on occasion. We are sometimes tempted to violate accepted norms when it is to our advantage and we sometimes yield to this temptation. These failings in our conduct do not imply that we do not accept the institution of morality, as is shown by the fact that violation of these norms is considered a legitimate basis for criticism—even by the violators. People express regrets, apologize, beg forgiveness, attempt to make amends, and so forth because they recognize they have done something wrong. Moral failings do not amount to a rejection of morality, nor do they imply that moral norms are not binding.

What if someone rejects the institution of morality altogether? The perceptive reader will not have failed to notice that I italicized "if" when a paragraph ago I stated, "*If* we accept the institution of morality, then we are tacitly agreeing to be bound by moral norms." I emphasized this condition precisely to draw attention to the fact that, as matter of logic, there is nothing preventing an individual from rejecting the institution of morality entirely, from "opting out" of morality as it were—that is, apart from the likely unpleasant consequences for that person of such a decision. There is nothing to be gained by pretending otherwise. There is no mystical intuition of "the moral law" that inexorably forces someone to accept the institution of morality. Nor is there any set of reasons whose irresistible logic compels a person to behave morally. Put another way, it is not irrational to reject the institution of morality altogether. One can coherently and consistently prefer what one regards as one's own self-interest to doing the morally appropriate thing. However, leaving aside those who suffer from a pathological lack of empathy, few choose this path. Among other things, this would be a difficult decision to make psychologically. As Hume observed, "Let a man's insensibility be ever so great, he must often be touched with the images of Right and Wrong" for "there is some benevolence, however small, that is infused into our bosom."[8] Furthermore, the consequence of rejecting morality entirely is to cut oneself off from human society.

That said, there is no guarantee people will not make this choice. But notice that bringing God into the picture doesn't change anything. People can make the decision to reject morality even if they think God has promulgated our shared moral norms. Indeed, many believers have made this decision, as evidenced by the individuals who throughout history have placed themselves outside the bounds of human society— hence becoming "outlaws"—and have sustained themselves by preying on other humans. Many ruthless brigands and pirates have had no doubts about God's existence. They still robbed, raped, and murdered anyway.

"But what they did was *objectively* wrong—and an atheist can't say this. As you have admitted, there is nothing outside the institution of morality to validate this institution, so the obligations of morality are not really binding."

If one means by "objectively wrong" something that conforms to a standard of wrongness that exists *completely* independently of the human condition and our moral practices, then, correct, an atheist might not use "objectively wrong" in this sense. (Some moralists who are atheists might, but that's another story.) But so what? First, as preceding chapters have suggested, the notion that God could provide such an external standard is highly questionable. Second, and more important, what is lost by acknowledging that morality is a wholly human phenomenon that arose to respond to the need to influence behavior so people can live together in peace? I would argue nothing is lost except some confused notions about morality that we would do well to discard.

Thought experiment: It is widely recognized that nonhuman animals are not regarded as being bound by moral norms. We don't blame the cat for killing the bird or for fighting with Tabby next door. Interaction between nonhuman animals is governed by tooth and claw, not moral norms. So no humans, no morality. Of course, in the absence of humans, there would still be rain, snow, and times without precipitation; there would still be night and day; the tides would still roll in and roll out; the laws of physics would still apply. There would be an infinite number of facts about the world even if there were no humans present. Yet there would be no morality. If we acknowledge that morality is an institution to address human concerns, an institution which reflects biological, psychological, and social facts *about humans*, then why would the contention that morality is an institution developed *by humans* result in such disquiet?

The temptation to think we need some standard external to morality to make morality objective and make moral obligations *really* binding is buttressed by the view that the only alternative is a subjectivist morality, but recognizing that morality is based on human needs and interests, and not God's commands, doesn't make one a subjectivist. When those who don't think that morality is derived from God say something is morally wrong, they don't (typically) mean this is just how they as individuals feel, which would be a true subjectivist position. One cannot argue with feelings. But most nonreligious think we *can* argue about moral issues and that some people are mistaken about their conclusions on moral matters.

To have genuine disagreements about moral issues, we need accepted standards for distinguishing correct from incorrect moral judgments and facts must influence our judgments. Morality as I have described it meets these conditions. All morally serious individuals accept the core moral norms I have identified, and it is these core norms that provide an intersubjective foundation for morality and for disagreements about more complex moral issues. For example, all morally serious individuals recognize there is a strong presumption that killing is wrong, and our knowledge that we live among others who also accept this norm allows us to venture outside instead of barricading ourselves in our homes.

However, the norm prohibiting killing by itself does not address more subtle issues, such as the issue of whether assisting someone to die is always morally wrong. To resolve this issue, we need some additional facts and we also need to reflect on the consequences of allowing such conduct and whether such consequences may be inconsistent with core norms and the objectives of morality. An answer may not be immediately obvious, but this in no way undercuts anyone's ability to claim their position is right and another person's is wrong. In other words, it does not imply morality is subjective. To the contrary, in making such judgments about controversial matters, people implicitly make reference to shared norms—which is what allows them to argue meaningfully with each other (until someone brings religious dogma into the conversation, which then stops it, as we have seen).

From the foregoing discussion, we can see that morality is not arbitrary. Moreover, people can argue intelligently about morality and can also assert that an action is morally wrong, not just for them, but wrong period. They can condemn wrongdoers, pointing out how their actions are inconsistent with core norms (although most wrongdoers are already aware of their transgressions). Furthermore, if the offense is serious enough, they will impose severe punishment on the wrongdoer, possibly including removal from society. All that seems pretty objective, in any relevant sense of the term. Granted, it's not objective in the same way that the statement that it is raining outside is objective, but that's because, as we have already established, factual statements have a different function than moral judgments.

At this point, the believer might protest, "But there has to be something more than that. Morality is not just a human institution." Well, what is this something more? Why is it not enough to tell the wrongdoer that everyone condemns him because what he did violated our accepted norms, which are essential to our ability to live together in peace? Do we have to add, "Oh, by the way, God condemns you too?" Exactly what difference would that make?

What some believers (and, again, some secular ethicists) appear to want is some further fact, something that will make them more comfortable in claiming that moral norms are authoritative and binding. Somehow it is not sufficient that a norm prohibiting the gratuitous affliction of violence reduces pain and suffering and allows us to live together in peace, and has, therefore, been adopted by all human societies. No, for the believer there has to be something else. A moral norm must be grounded in something other than its beneficial effects for humans and human communities. The statement that "it was wrong for Sam to hit Chris" must pick out some mystical property that constitutes "wrongness." For the believer, this further fact is usually identified as a command from God, but as we have already established, God's commands cannot be regarded as imposing moral obligations unless we already possess a sense of right and wrong independent of his commands.

Those who cling to the "further fact" view—that is, the view that there must be something outside of morality that provides the objective grounding for morality—are not unlike those naive economists who insist that currency has no value unless it's based on gold or some other precious metal. Hence, we had the gold standard which for many years provided that a dollar could be exchanged for a specific quantity of gold. The gold standard reassured some that currency was based on something of "objective" value. However, the whole world has moved away from the gold standard with no ill effects. Why was there no panic? Why didn't our economic systems collapse or become wildly unstable? Because currency doesn't need anything outside of the economic system itself to provide it with value. Money represents the value found *within* our economic system, which, in turn, is based on our economic relationships.

Similarly, moral norms represent the value found in living together. There is no need to base our moral norms on something outside of our relationships. Moral norms are effective in fostering collaboration and cooperation, in improving our conditions, and there is no need to refer to a mystical entity, a gold bar, or God to conclude that we should encourage everyone to abide by common moral norms.

In conclusion, the claim that we need God to provide morality with objectivity does not withstand analysis. To begin, God would not be able to provide objectivity, as explained in the previous chapter. Moreover, morality is neither objective nor subjective in the way statements of fact are said to be objective or subjective, nor is that type of objectivity really our concern. Our legitimate concern is that we don't want people feeling free "to do their own thing," that is, we don't want morality to be merely a reflection of someone's personal desires. It's not. To the extent intersubjective validity is required for morality, it is provided by the fact that, in relevant respects, the circumstances under which humans live have remained roughly the same. We have similar vulnerabilities and needs to people who lived in ancient times and medieval times and to people who live today in other parts of the world. The obligation to tell the truth will persist as long as humans need to rely on communications from each other. The obligation to assist those who are in need of food and water will persist as long as humans need hydration and nutrition to sustain themselves. The obligation not to maim someone will persist as long as humans cannot spontaneously heal wounds and regrow body parts. The obligation not to kill someone will persist as long as we lack the power of reanimation. In its essentials, the human condition has not changed much, and it is the circumstances under which we live that influence the content of our norms, not divine commands.

Religion Not a Source of Universal Moral Norms

It is somewhat ironic that God is so often identified as the guarantor of a morality that is unquestionably binding on all of us, regardless of our beliefs or nationality, when religiously based codes of conduct have so often promoted a limited, parochial viewpoint, that is, the viewpoint of the adherents of a particular faith. As noted, there is a core of moral norms that humans have shared throughout history. That is the common morality, and we don't need God for that. But there have also been many norms that are peculiar to a given culture. Many of these norms deal with religious practices and reflect a tribal outlook. Most gods have been the gods of particular groups of people. One significant function of religiously based norms has been to reinforce group solidarity by mandating practices and behaviors that serve to distinguish a god's "chosen people" from infidels.

Anyone with a passing familiarity with a couple of different religions can list dozens of norms that are peculiar to a given religion.

Don't eat certain food; don't drink certain beverages; don't prepare or serve food or beverages in certain ways; don't wear certain clothing; don't create, possess, or display certain artwork; don't say certain words; don't dye your hair certain colors; don't worship in certain ways; don't work on certain days; don't dispose of human remains in certain ways; refrain from certain sexual practices; and on and on—the list of taboos is lengthy. For some of the taboos of Judaism see Exod. 21–23 and the entire book of Leviticus. These taboos are intended to be taken seriously, as seriously as any of the divine commandments that reflect universal moral norms, such as "You shall not steal." The prescribed penalty for breaking many of these taboos is death. Yet the relationship of these taboos to human welfare and the reduction of social conflict is remote at best.

These religious norms not only fail to promote human welfare; they also have actually served to limit benevolence. They promote in-group solidarity while fostering hostility to outsiders. As Jonathan Haidt has observed, "Religion is … well suited to be the handmaiden of groupishness, tribalism, and nationalism."[9] Norms dealing with cultic practice are especially prone to promote conflict as they are often strikingly intolerant. The ancient Israelites were commanded to invade the land of the Canaanites and other tribes in part because of the different religious practices of these tribes; this was also the motivation for God's unequivocal, merciless instruction to slaughter these tribes and destroy their places of worship—they were worshipping in the wrong way (see, for example, Deut. 20: 16–18). Of course, the conflicts caused by religion-specific codes of conduct are not just ancient history. Animosities fueled by God's revelations about how he wants to be worshipped and what cultic practices he requires continue today. The many attacks against alleged blasphemers in countries such as Pakistan and Afghanistan illustrate how many still perceive God as a being who becomes enraged at the slightest offense, even when committed inadvertently. These animosities are found within religions as well as between religions because of the different interpretations given to the same revelation. A recent comical example of such disputes (comical because, fortunately, no one was seriously hurt) is the December 2011 broom fight that broke out between Orthodox Christian clerics—one group Greek, one Armenian—at the Church of the Nativity.[10]

Religion has been useful as a means of inculcating moral norms, as I have previously noted. That said, religion has not made a worthwhile contribution to the content of moral norms. Some norms endorsed by religious groups are acceptable; they are acceptable because they are similar to the core set of norms that constitute the common morality. We would have these norms anyway regardless of their endorsement by a particular religion. We do not need the Ten Commandments to tell us it is wrong to lie or to steal. We have these norms because they enable us to fulfill the objectives of morality. The unique contributions that religion has made to the content of moral norms have been either neutral or negative in value. Religion-specific norms promote practices that are pointless or harmful—harmful because, among other things, they restrict individual autonomy and foster animosity to those outside the faith. Looking to a particular religion for guidance on moral questions is at best an inefficient use of time and at worst an exercise that will severely distort one's moral compass.

A claim frequently made by believers is that religious teachings have provided the impetus for certain transformational changes in our moral outlook. This claim is false. To the extent this claim has a kernel of truth, it is based on an equivocation between religious teachings as a general source of inspiration and religious teachings as a specific source of moral norms. There have been some revolutionary changes in moral outlook, most of which have occurred in the last few centuries. Two stand out in particular, namely the end to slavery and the emancipation of women. One would think that if God provides us with objectively valid moral norms that are universally applicable, he would have made clear his opposition to slavery and the subordination of women long ago. That wasn't the case. Moreover, when we examine these moral revolutions, we see that religiously based norms were not instrumental in bringing about change.

To understand how these important changes in moral outlook came about, and to understand the role of religion in these changes, we should first examine how the changes can be accommodated by my claim that there is a common morality, that is, a set of core moral norms that have been shared by all cultures. Slavery is universally condemned nowadays, but it was an accepted social practice in most past cultures. How then can I claim there is a common morality?

To begin, as indicated in the previous section of this chapter, we need to distinguish between the content of a norm and the scope of the norm, that is, the range of individuals to whom the norm applies. The revolutionary transformations in morality that have taken place have not changed the content of core norms, but they have broadened the class of individuals who are entitled to moral respect. Norms such as do not kill, do not steal, and tell the truth have been part of the moral code of all functioning human communities, but early in the history of humanity, these communities were small. Furthermore, the constraints imposed by morality did not apply to those outside one's community. The tribe down the valley was viewed as a threat—usually because they were a threat—not as potential collaborators. Warfare was incessant, and was carried out with brutality.[11] Those outside one's tribe or clan were entitled to little or no moral respect, with victors in these conflicts routinely massacring or enslaving those who were defeated and taking possession of their material goods.

Slavery was a byproduct of these struggles—to the extent that the conquering tribe could manage its captives (if it could not, they were killed). Historians agree both that the initial source of slaves was warfare and that almost all ancient cultures had slaves.[12]

In other words, slavery was what happened to those outside the moral community—aliens, barbarians, and so forth. As one historian has noted, "because it was difficult to treat men of one's own tribe as no more than animals, the survival of true slavery required some form of social or psychological discrimination."[13] The sad fact is that humanity was not one big happy family in the distant past; there was no concept of universal human rights.

Religion is not to be blamed for this. It's simply a reflection of how human communities evolved. On the other hand, religion did little to help eliminate these divisions. Instead, religion took these divisions for granted and developed codes that distinguished between those who were favored by God and those who were outsiders. The outsiders were candidates for slavery. The critical importance of "otherness" can be discerned from God's admonition to Moses that slavery is permissible, but only for those individuals "from among the nations that are around you [and] from among the strangers who sojourn with you" (Lev. 25: 44–45). Similarly, in Islamic countries, Muslims could enslave non-Muslims. They did not possess the same moral status as Muslims.

Slavery became embedded within the social structure in much of the ancient world. The generation of economic surplus and, therefore, wealth depended upon it. Slavery persisted in the Roman Empire and, thereafter, its remnants up through the early Middle Ages. It was rarely questioned. Chattel slavery did decrease in medieval Europe, but principally because of economic conditions, not enlightenment brought about by Christianity. Although the Church condemned enslavement of fellow Christians, "these scruples . . . did not extend to unbelievers who were usually thought to be undeserving of freedom." [14] In fact, on occasion, the Church encouraged Christians to enslave unbelievers. In 1452, Pope Nicholas V issued his bull *Dum Diversas*, which granted the king of Portugal the right to subdue Saracens, pagans, and other unbelievers and "reduce them to perpetual slavery."[15] Soon thereafter, the Portuguese began large-scale slaving expeditions into Africa, just in time to acquire slaves for work in the Americas.

Organized opposition to slavery did not take shape until the mid-eighteenth century, starting in the United Kingdom, a country, perhaps not coincidentally, that had no slaves—except in its colonies.[16] This significant change in attitude had many causes, but among them were the growing acceptance in some European countries and the newly founded United States of the notion of fundamental rights possessed by all men (and men is the proper word here) and the gradual recognition that some of the justifications for enslavement of Africans—such as their supposed inherent intellectual inferiority—had no factual support. At some point, a critical mass of people ceased to see the slave, and those African communities that were the source of slaves, as wholly "other." Instead, they regarded these individuals as part of the moral community to whom the same level of moral respect should be granted, and, consequently, this implied they should no longer be enslaved. Abolition spread from Europe to the Americas and then, slowly, around the globe. The United Nations Universal Declaration of Human Rights, adopted in 1948, prohibited slavery; in 1981, Mauritania became the last country to abolish slavery.[17]

What were the contributions of religion to this transformational change in outlook? Very little. As indicated, slavery is expressly authorized by the Old Testament. The New Testament and the Qur'an do not forbid it, and until modern times the Catholic Church condemned only enslavement of fellow Christians. Thus, slavery was permissible according to the precepts of the major monotheistic religions.

We can see then that some of the claims that have been made about the importance of religion for abolishing slavery are unwarranted. If Christianity prohibited slavery, it took over 1,800 years for most Christians to realize this. Admittedly, much of the abolitionist rhetoric was phrased in religious language, but so too were proslavery pamphlets and speeches.[18] One of the arguments for slavery in the antebellum South was precisely that it exposed Africans to Christianity, thereby giving slaves an opportunity to save their souls that otherwise would not have been available to them. In the midst of the Civil War, Southern clergy issued "An Address to Christians Throughout the World," in which they appealed for an end to the fighting and, with the support of several scriptural citations, argued not only that slavery was justified, but also that the abolition of slavery would interfere with "Divine Providence."[19]

I am not denying here that many abolitionists found inspiration in the Bible. To repeat myself, religion has been the principal vehicle used to inculcate moral norms for most of human history, and it is to be expected that individuals in a culture where religion predominated would utilize religious imagery and metaphors in making arguments against slavery. But religion was not the source of the change in moral perspective. It is not as though some cleric woke up one morning and said, "Goodness, we've been interpreting the Bible incorrectly all along." No, people first began to see the African as human, as a full member of the moral community, and this change in moral outlook was then couched in the moral language of the day, which was religious in nature. In sum, religion was not responsible for the change in moral perspective that brought about the end of slavery. If anything, it retarded development of that perspective.

Something similar can be said for the other major transformational change in our moral outlook that has taken place in the last couple of centuries, and that is the change in moral status of women. If anything, with respect to this moral revolution, religion has acted as even more of a brake on change than it did in the case of slavery.

The moral status of women in past cultures is more complex than that of the barbarian outsider who was a candidate for slavery. Women were inside the moral community and, for obvious reasons, regarded as valuable. They were essential for the community's survival. So they were within the scope of the community's moral norms. Nonetheless, they had a subordinate status to men and did not enjoy the same rights or protections as men. The origins and explanation for this subordinate status remain unclear and disputed; for example, some scholars have argued that women did not have a subordinate status in some hunter-gatherer societies. These controversies need not detain us here. What is beyond dispute is that in societies for which we have historical records, women did not have the same status as men. They were obliged to submit to the authority of their fathers or husbands; their rights to possess property were restricted; most occupations were closed to them; their sex lives were rigidly controlled; their political rights were limited; education—don't even ask. This situation persisted for millennia. A woman's status in sixteenth century England was only marginally different from a woman's status in Sumer in 2500 BCE.

Religion cannot be blamed for initiating the subordination of women, no more than it can be blamed for slavery. As with slavery, though, religion has helped perpetuate the second-class status of women. The sacred scriptures of Judaism, Christianity, and Islam all prescribe an inferior status for women and depict this inferior status as a divine mandate. To say it has been an article of faith that women are inferior to men is no mere figure of speech. Interestingly, in 1890 the number of people in the United States "who believed the Bible sanctioned woman suffrage was far smaller than the number of people who, in 1830, thought it condemned slavery."[20] In fact, the Bible was invoked repeatedly by opponents of women's rights throughout the nineteenth and early twentieth centuries. In his notorious concurring opinion in *Bradwell v. State*—which upheld an Illinois ban on women practicing law—Supreme Court Justice Joseph Bradley reasoned, "The constitution of the family organization, which is founded in the divine ordinance ... indicates the domestic sphere as that which properly belongs to the domain and functions of womanhood. ... This is the law of the Creator."[21] Religious doctrines have continued to provide justification for the subordination of women up to the present day; indeed, in some Islamic countries these doctrines provide the justification for horrific acts of violence against women who have, in some way, violated the restrictions imposed on their conduct.[22]

Moreover, unlike the struggle against slavery, in which some religious leaders featured prominently, the struggle against the subordination of women has been led by a mix of religious and secular reformers. Furthermore, the arguments for women's rights and gender equality have been based largely on secular considerations. For example, the arguments for women's suffrage were based largely on a claim of equal rights and the need for the franchise to protect the interests of women.[23] Many of those who pushed for reform were religious skeptics. Mary Wollstonecraft, the author of *A Vindication of the Rights of Women* and a feminist pioneer, was a religious skeptic. So too was Elizabeth Cady Stanton, arguably the leading American advocate for women's rights in the nineteenth century.[24] One of the most influential essays on women's rights, *On the Subjection of Women*, was written by two agnostics, John Stuart Mill and Harriet Taylor.[25] Robert Ingersoll, the renowned nineteenth-century American orator, was a passionate advocate of women's rights in addition to being an atheist.[26] This is not to say that there have been no religious individuals or groups who have been involved in advocating for women's rights. Of course there have been. In the United States, the Women's Christian Temperance Union was one of the most influential groups that worked for suffrage (although one reason it did so was to have enough votes to pass laws prohibiting alcohol). But, for the most part, the arguments that have been advanced on behalf of women's rights have not been based on religious doctrines; instead, they have been advanced in the face of religious doctrines.

The radical change in moral perspective that, in developed countries, eventually removed many (not necessarily all) of the legal and social restrictions on women was the result of several different factors. Among these were the tireless efforts of advocates for women's rights— some of whom sacrificed their lives—the gradual erosion of prejudice through factual evidence that women could work successfully in any profession and were capable of reasoning about political issues as well as men, and changes in economic conditions that provided greater opportunities for women to enter the work force. In this connection, the First World War proved a watershed. Millions of women took on the jobs left vacant by men who were serving in the armed forces.[27] It's not a coincidence that women achieved the right to vote in the United States, the United Kingdom, and Germany shortly after the war.

We cannot say with certainty which of these many factors was the most critical for the shift in moral perspective that allowed us to see women as the equals of men. We can say with certainty that religion was not one of the factors.

The notion that God speaks to us through revealed religion to instruct us on timeless, objectively valid moral norms is decisively refuted by the role that religion played with respect to slavery and the subordination of women. Those who claim that God speaks to us and instructs us on moral issues must concede that he did not whisper a note of opposition to slavery and the subordination of women for millennia. To the contrary, these practices had the full support of religious institutions. When change finally did come, religion was either a source of conflicting opinions (slavery) or primarily a source of resistance (women's rights). Granted, many, but certainly far from all, religious institutions have now entered the twenty-first century, and they accept the full equality of all humans. All this shows is that religion can sometimes play catch-up. God supposedly guarantees moral objectivity because he gives us fixed standards. The more realistic way to look at this issue is to acknowledge that religious institutions get fixed in their positions, which often makes them resistant to change and moral reform, precisely because they base their codes on God's supposed revelations—for how can God's message change?

The Rigidity of Religiously Based Norms

The foregoing section describes how the notion of divinely fixed standards has inhibited needed moral reforms. Another way in which the notion of God's fixed standards has been detrimental to a proper understanding of morality is with respect to the claim that morality deals with "absolutes"—in other words, there are certain actions that are always forbidden. Moral prohibitions are "absolutes" because they are exceptionless. On this view, acts such as lying or stealing or adultery (or for some Catholics, contraception) are always wrong no matter what the consequences. Supposedly, this interpretation of moral norms shows the advantage of a morality based on divine commands. Some theists argue that if appeals to God are ruled out, then it is not possible to establish the existence of moral absolutes and—somehow—this is an outcome to be dreaded.[28]

To the contrary, this concern about "absolutes," much like the worries about "objectivity," displays a fundamental misunderstanding of the moral enterprise. Moral norms do not function as absolutes, and anyone with significant life experience is aware of this, at least on an intuitive level. Insisting that there are moral absolutes creates needless dilemmas and interferes with clear thinking about morality. In turn, this leads to unyielding stances on certain points in public policy disputes, with serious adverse consequences for the formulation of sound, beneficial public policy. (In chapter 7, where I discuss legalization of assisted dying, the public policy consequences of thinking in terms of moral absolutes will become apparent.)

Before tackling the issue of moral absolutes head-on, let us first think about moral norms and how they function. We acknowledge, and try to conform our behavior to, various moral norms. For most of us, the number of norms we can identify at any one time is small, maybe a dozen or so. But the fact that we can specifically identify only a small number of norms should not trouble us. As a practical manner, being habituated to act in certain ways requires the number of norms to be small. We could not inculcate morality successfully in children if moral codes were as complex as legal codes. (As an aside, we can see how religious taboos guarantee employment for a clerical class. No human involved in the business of living has time to memorize a religion's myriad restrictions on food, beverages, apparel, personal hygiene, and so forth. So these become the province of the rabbi, priest, or imam.) Furthermore, a small number of norms is sufficient, because as we acquire moral maturity, we learn to balance our obligations and resolve dilemmas.

Norms can conflict. This is a reality that the absolutists struggle to deny. As we mature and gain experience, we learn how to deal with these conflicts and resolve them in such a way that the objectives of morality are furthered, not frustrated.

Consider a simple example. You are a professor who has promised a student that you will meet with him at 5:00 p.m. It is important to him that you not be late because he has to go to his part-time job at 6:00. This is a commitment you should keep; you are morally obliged to do so. Failure to keep the commitment because you just do not feel like it or you want to continue chatting with a colleague would be wrong. Let us suppose, though, that on your way to your office you cross a parking lot where there is a body of an elderly man lying face down on the pavement. Few others are around; moreover, no one else is doing anything. Should you stop to see if the person needs help? And, if so, should you not make some effort to help the person, for example, by placing a 911 call and waiting for help to arrive? And should you not do this even if it makes you miss your appointment?

The answers to these questions are obvious to any morally serious person. One of our accepted norms is to help others in distress when we can do so without endangering ourselves or others. Moreover, we know from our experience and the ability to make moral judgments which we have developed that saving a life takes precedence over the prior commitment to meet the student. It is not that you did not have an obligation to meet the student. You did. However, you have an overriding obligation to try to assist the person who is face down in the parking lot.

This is how we should regard our moral norms, that is, as imposing obligations that can conflict and that we may need to balance. In practice, it is also the way in which we do regard our moral norms, at least for those whose judgment is not warped by a dogmatic approach to ethics. Our norms impose obligations, but these obligations can be overridden by other obligations. In the words of the twentieth-century English ethicist W. D. Ross, our norms impose *prima facie* obligations, that is, they impose obligations that must be followed *unless* there is a competing norm that imposes an obligation that takes priority.[29]

How do we determine which norms have priority? A utilitarian might claim we can do a precise calculation of the happiness, pleasure, or well-being that would be produced by alternative courses of action. I am doubtful of our capacity to make such calculations. However, although we might not achieve the utilitarian's dream of a moral calculus, we are capable of making a rough weighing of harms and benefits based on our knowledge of human needs and interests. We have no difficulty determining that in ordinary circumstances saving a life takes precedence over keeping an appointment, just as we have no trouble determining that breaking into someone's cabin and eating their food is permissible if I have been lost in the woods for three days. Under these circumstances, my obligation to preserve my life takes priority over the obligation to refrain from stealing and damaging someone else's property. We have an obligation to tell the truth, but if I have chosen to engage in espionage for my country, it is understood I will engage in deceit routinely because this obligation is overridden by my commitment to protect my fellow citizens against those who are trying to harm them. I have an obligation to remain sexually faithful to my spouse, but if I have to commit adultery to save my spouse's life—perhaps because this is the price to free him from those holding him hostage—this action is permissible.

From the examples I have given, and from our common moral sense, one can readily see that preservation of life usually takes priority over other obligations. The prohibition on killing is at the core of our morality, for obvious reasons. We need life to be able to accomplish anything, enjoy anything. Preserving a person's life is necessary for that person to partake of friendship, fall in love, obtain knowledge, work on personal projects, and so on. There is a strong, almost irrefutable, presumption that killing another human is immoral. That great weight is placed on our norm prohibiting killing is understandable. Unfortunately, for many religious institutions and individuals, this norm has been interpreted in absolutist terms, causing needless difficulties in moral analysis as well as serious harm.

For some religious bodies and individuals, the norm "do not kill" is applied as is, with no modification. This is the position of religious pacifists. Most religious bodies and individuals, however, build exceptions into the rule so the rule is transformed from the straightforward "do not kill" into "do not take innocent life." The qualification of "innocent life" is inserted in the norm to allow for killing in self-defense, including in wartime situations, and capital punishment—at least for those religious who still support capital punishment. (In the last few decades, capital punishment has become another issue that has divided believers, resulting in scriptural quotes being hurled back and forth.) Defenders of the qualified norm argue that, properly modified, the norm is now truly exceptionless, and taking an innocent life is always forbidden. In the words of Pope John Paul II, "The deliberate decision to deprive an innocent human being of life is always morally evil and can never be licit [even] as a means to a good end."[30]

The "sanctity-of-life" principle is the name usually given to this absolutist position. This principle has been invoked in a number of policy disputes, including disputes over the cessation of life-sustaining treatment. Although most of the religious opposition to withdrawal or withholding of life-sustaining treatment has now faded, in the 1970s and early 1980s, many religious individuals and groups, especially the Catholic Church, opposed legal recognition of the right of patients or their surrogates to refuse life-sustaining treatment, at least when this treatment was considered "ordinary" as opposed to "extraordinary." This resulted in unnecessary prolongation of life and increased the suffering of patients and/or their loved ones. Legalization was made possible only after the adoption of a convenient legal fiction by which the physician or other healthcare professional who ceases the treatment only intends to respect the patient's wishes; he does not intend the patient's death.[31] It is fortunate that the right to refuse treatment is now well established in many countries; it is unfortunate that it took a long struggle to obtain this right and that it was achieved at the price of indulging in moral and legal sophistry.

Life is good. But in extreme circumstances such as when a patient is in a persistent vegetative state or is conscious but enduring immense suffering, life can lose its value. In such cases, when a patient has either contemporaneously or by advance directive indicated a desire to cease treatment, forcing the patient to remain alive because of the "sanctity of life" is effectively to appropriate that person's life for the sake of dogma. Anyone not blinded by dogma could see that compassion and respect for the patient's wishes can, in such extreme circumstances, override our obligations to preserve life. All too often, religiously based codes do not have the flexibility to permit this balancing of our obligations. The deity's absolute directives prevent consideration of human interests and needs.

In sum: this chapter has shown that there is no need for God to serve as the commissioner of morality. Moral rules do not become less binding when we recognize they are a human creation. Furthermore, the notion of fixed standards imposed by God has impeded moral reform while also interfering with day-to-day moral reasoning. Instead of focusing on whether our actions serve the objectives of morality, the divine command theory requires us to conform our actions to rigid rules that too often are divorced from the realities of life.

* * * *

We now turn in the next chapter to the role of God as moral enforcer—the last refuge for those who maintain God is indispensable for morality.

Six

MORALITY WITHOUT A SUPERNATURAL NET

Many people believe there is a necessary connection between God—more properly, belief in God—and the motivation to act morally. Indeed, when one refers to God being necessary or indispensable for morality, it is this relationship that most often springs to mind. This belief is deeply embedded in the worldview of many religious individuals. This connection is also endorsed—repeatedly—by many religious leaders and theologians. Moreover, one finds echoes of this viewpoint both in literature and in popular culture. It is fair to say it is a common belief. Those holding this viewpoint maintain that if people come to believe there is no God overseeing their conduct—punishing them for bad deeds and rewarding them for good deeds— then they will always act in their own self-interest.

Not only is this belief currently widespread, but it also has deep historical roots. Before the last couple of centuries, it would be difficult to find many who challenged this view. Even those who thought morality is not based directly on God's commands usually believed God was needed as a moral enforcer. We saw earlier that John Locke, who believed in natural rights, also was of the opinion that we had no obligation to tolerate atheists because atheists could not be trusted: oaths were meaningless to them. Interestingly, some atheists also have thought that God serves an indispensable role as a moral motivator— at least for many people. Critias, a student of Socrates and a reputed atheist—and later one of the infamous Thirty Tyrants—has had attributed to him the following excerpt from a play:

> A time there was when anarchy did rule
> The lives of men, which were then like the beasts,
> Enslaved to force; nor was there then reward
> For good men, nor for wicked punishment.
> . . . .
> Next, as the laws did hold men back from deeds
> Of open violence, but still such deeds
> Were done in secret, then, as I maintain
> Some shrewd man first, a man in counsel wise,
> Discovered unto men the fear of Gods,
> Thereby to frighten sinners should they sin
> E'en secretly in deed, or word, or thought.
> Hence was it that he brought in Deity
> Telling how God enjoys an endless life,
> Hears with his mind and sees, and taketh thought
> And heeds things, and his nature is divine,
> So that he harkens to men's every word
> And has the power to see men's every act.[1]

In other words, God is an invention, but a necessary one. Laws help control our behavior, but only when there is a risk one will be observed. An all-seeing, all-knowing God is required to keep us in line, especially when we are out of public view.

From the foregoing, it is readily apparent that a large number of people have been and are attached to this viewpoint. This does not imply it has any support in logic or fact, however.

Before assessing the merits of this view, I want to point out one reason many contemporary believers doggedly cling to this view. We live in an era where some of the traditional arguments for God's existence have lost much of their persuasive power. For example, the argument from design, that is, the argument that we need God to explain why there is a universe and why humans are part of that universe, used to be widely accepted; cosmology, evolutionary biology, and science in general have deprived this argument of its appeal. We just do not need God anymore to fill in the gaps of our knowledge. Whether they will concede this or not, believers are on the intellectual defensive. But if belief in God is necessary to motivate people to act morally, then this provides the believer with a rhetorical foothold to argue for belief in God. As a matter of logic, of course, even if belief in God were required to motivate people to act morally, this would not prove there is a God. However, it could establish that one should encourage belief in God, assuming we do not want society to unravel due to unconstrained egoism. In terms of arguing for belief in God, this may be the best card left for the theist to play. He is not going to give it up easily.

Let us look at this contention, then. As with some other claims we have examined, distinctions can and should be made between variants of the claim. The two principal variants are these: (1) the individual atheist is less likely to behave morally than the individual believer; and (2) disbelief in God may have no immediate perceptible effect, but over time, especially if the number of nonbelievers increases, it will inevitably lead to a loss in the influence of moral norms—in other words, the issue is not the effect of disbelief on isolated individuals, but its long-term effects on society. This latter claim is the more credible of the two, not so much because there is any evidence to confirm it, but because it is essentially a prediction about the future, so there is little evidence to refute it.

God, Morality, and the Individual Atheist

"Anybody that doesn't believe in God isn't a good citizen, and if an atheist found a wallet on the ground they would pick it up, plunder the money, and throw the wallet back on the ground."[2] This quote, attributed to a local Boy Scouts leader commenting on the expulsion of an atheist scout, captures nicely the image many have of the moral character of atheists. It certainly expresses succinctly the attitude of the Boy Scouts of America (BSA) toward atheists. The BSA regards atheists as unfit for scouting, and they have expelled a number of boys and young men who were in good standing with the scouts—some were Eagle Scouts—solely because of their lack of belief in God. There is no legal impediment to this blatant discrimination by the BSA because supposedly it is a "private organization," albeit a private organization enjoying substantial support from public resources. Therefore, it is permitted to establish its own rules for membership. But regardless of whether the BSA is a private organization, where is the outrage over its exclusionary membership policy? If the BSA were to exclude Jews, Mormons, or Muslims, do you think the organization would have access to public lands for their jamborees or have commemorative postage stamps issued in the organization's honor?

The BSA can continue to exclude the nonreligious without fear of any significant protest from the public—it's principally nonbelievers along with a few fair-minded believers who have complained about the BSA membership policy—because, sadly, the prejudice of the organization reflects the prejudice of many Americans. Similarly, few prominent political figures have denounced the organization because politicians either support the policy or they fear the public backlash if they were to denounce the organization's policy.

Survey after survey confirms that close to half of Americans find atheists untrustworthy. About 43 percent of Americans consider atheists unfit for the presidency—even if otherwise qualified.[3] This distrust of atheists also extends to the personal sphere. In a revealing 2006 study, researchers at the University of Minnesota determined that over 47 percent of Americans would disapprove if their child married an atheist (compared to a 33 percent disapproval rate for marriage to a Muslim).[4] The authors of the study concluded that American tolerance for religious diversity does not extend to atheists, who are viewed as lacking moral values shared by other Americans. As part of the study, in-depth interviews were conducted with a portion of the survey respondents. These interviews revealed that atheists were associated with "illegality, such as drug use and prostitution—that is, immoral people who threaten respectable community."[5] One interviewee stated that "prisons are probably filled with people who don't have any kind of spiritual or religious core."[6] In the formal conclusion to their report, the researchers stated:

> The core point of this article can be stated concisely. Atheists are at the top of the list of groups that Americans find problematic in both public and private life, and the gap between acceptance of atheists and acceptance of other racial and religious minorities is large and persistent.[7]

Let me conclude this overview of how atheists are regarded by many Americans with a couple of personal anecdotes, which will confirm the extent to which some view atheists with suspicion. As I have mentioned, I worked for most of my professional life as a lawyer. For my entire legal career, I worked in the Washington, DC office of a major national law firm. The law firm attracted graduates of the nation's top law schools, in other words, people presumptively intelligent.

We didn't discuss religion much at the firm, for the reasons most people don't discuss religion at work—it has no relevance to their jobs. However, I didn't hide the fact that I was an atheist, and this fact became known to some of the lawyers and staff at the firm.

A lawyer joined the firm about ten years after I did. Within a few months, we became friends for the best of reasons for lawyers—we both did good work and we could rely on each other for assistance with cases. Anyway, about two years later, around the time of the firm's holiday party, my friend learned I was an atheist. She stopped in front of my office door with a dazed look. "Ron Lindsay is an atheist. Ron Lindsay is an atheist," she repeated with astonishment.

As she explained, my friend initially had trouble processing the fact that I didn't believe in God because I was "such a nice guy." She didn't think amiability and atheism were compatible. However, she admitted she had not been well-acquainted with many atheists, as she had been raised in a religious household and had attended parochial schools.

This is a highly intelligent person who had seven years of higher education, including three years of law school. She eventually became a partner in this firm.

I relate this incident because it illustrates that, at least in the United States, myths about nonbelievers are not confined to the uneducated or those who live in small-town America. Granted, higher education and living in a metropolitan area may make it more likely that you will not view atheists with suspicion, but that's principally because in those circumstances, you're more likely to come into contact with nonbelievers. To a large extent, prejudice toward nonbelievers is a function of two things: the extent to which one has been told that atheists are bad people and the level of one's familiarity with open nonbelievers. If you are repeatedly told for most of your life that atheists are immoral and untrustworthy and you never have the opportunity to know an atheist personally, there is a strong likelihood that a negative image of atheists will continue to guide your outlook.

The irony is that many people who are prejudiced against atheists probably *are* acquainted with atheists—they are just not aware of this. One reason they are not aware of this is because many nonbelievers remain closeted. They have not revealed their skepticism to relatives, friends, or colleagues because they are concerned about the reaction they will receive, and with good reason.

This is the Catch-22 for nonbelievers. Prejudice against them persists in part because they do not let it be known they are nonbelievers, and this reluctance to come out of the closet persists in part because of the prejudice against nonbelievers.

In using the term "prejudice" to describe the attitude that some believers have toward atheists, I don't mean to imply that these believers are evil or stupid. No, in using "prejudice" I am adhering to the original sense of the term, which connotes a judgment made without being aware of the relevant facts. I would not call believers who have a low regard for atheists stupid or evil, because I had a dim view of atheists once myself. I thought atheists were horrible people, based on ... well, based on nothing. This belief was the product, not of evidence, but of the supposedly essential link between God and good behavior being drummed into my head for many years combined with my lack of acquaintance with atheists. Before I went to college, I knew exactly two atheists, a married couple. They were neighbors who, like my family, lived in the quarters provided to professional staff at the veteran's medical center where my father worked. The couple was of mixed Dutch-Indonesian ancestry, which, of course, to my adolescent sensibilities complemented their professed atheism: they were weird outsiders. I was about thirteen when I learned of their strange beliefs by witnessing a conversation between them and my parents. I was shocked: it was like seeing the devil in the flesh. Anyway, it led to some prolonged praying on my part—praying that I can still recall with some shame decades later. The couple had a young daughter, so because I was aghast and alarmed at the prospect of this young child being raised by people with no moral values, I asked God to have her taken away from this couple. I don't recall requesting that any specific plan of action be implemented. I left that to God's discretion and infinite wisdom. Anyway, nothing happened. Their daughter remained with them, and no thunderbolts struck our neighborhood. One reason I recall this episode with some clarity is because after I became an atheist, I married and had two children myself. I sometimes wondered how many people thought I could not be a fit parent.

So I can understand why some believers look upon atheists with suspicion. They don't know any better, just like I didn't know any better. Of course, this doesn't justify their attitude. To justify their attitude there would have to be some evidence that atheists behave badly more often than believers. There is no such evidence.

There is no reliable study showing nonbelievers are more likely to engage in dishonest, immoral, or criminal conduct. Do atheists lie or cheat? Of course they do, but no more frequently than believers. For example, a classic 1975 study of cheating among college students ("Faith Without Works: Jesus People, Resistance to Temptation, and Altruism") determined that there was no difference in the "frequency or magnitude" of cheating between religious and nonreligious students.[8] Subsequent studies have confirmed this result.[9]

If atheists were more inclined to engage in bad behavior, they should be vastly overrepresented in prisons. As indicated in chapter 4, that is not true in the United States, at least based on some informal surveys. In fact, atheists are underrepresented in the prison population. Of course, if there are relatively few atheists in prisons, this implies the overwhelming majority of felons are theists. So not only does lack of belief not turn one into a criminal, but religious belief does not prevent one from becoming a criminal.

The notion that lack of belief in God is going to transform someone into an unscrupulous cheat or felon is based on a serious misunderstanding of human moral psychology. Our conduct has three primary determinants: our biology, the influences to which we are exposed as we are growing up, and the reinforcement certain desirable character traits receive through the praise/blame mechanisms of the moral community. Excepting psychopaths (who do account for a disproportionate share of the prison population), our evolutionary heritage has disposed us to feel empathy and to act benevolently.[10] Moreover, if we are raised properly, we are habituated to act in accordance with the common morality. Parents have always worried about their children hanging out with "the wrong crowd"—and they have reason to worry, because in our early years our character is especially susceptible to being shaped by external forces. Once our character is formed, for better or worse, it's not likely to change radically as we age. To be sure, even as adults we remain susceptible to good and bad influences. To ensure our habits of virtue are sustained after we become adults—and also to nudge those who may not have the best character—our good actions are praised and our bad actions are condemned or punished by the moral community. This combination of influences largely accounts for our conduct. What doesn't seem to matter much is the nature of our metaphysical beliefs, for example, whether we believe in God. Ceasing to believe in God is unlikely to produce much change in our character or everyday conduct. We don't need God to behave morally. We just need to keep doing what we have been doing as humans for thousands of years. We can have morality without a supernatural net.

Some may challenge my assertion that a change in metaphysical beliefs, that is, a change in one's views about the ultimate nature of things, is unlikely to affect one's character or everyday conduct. They may point to people who do horrible things because they are prompted to do so by their religious beliefs—for example, the 9/11 terrorists. But my claim relates to *everyday* conduct. Persons may be persuaded to fly airplanes into buildings because of their belief in a God who demands *jihad*, but the day-to-day conduct of Islamic terrorists is not markedly different from the conduct of other people. They pay their bills, they share food, they are polite to people, they do not steal (except when required for their mission), and so forth. Fanatics devoted to a religion or to an ideology will be willing to sacrifice human life to achieve whatever goals they think their God or creed demands, but at the same time they may be "kind to children," as Hitler supposedly was. Fanaticism, religious or ideological, does not make one thoroughly immoral.

Instead, it blinds one to the humanity of one's opponents, imagined or real. Robbed of moral status, the infidels, subhumans, or enemies of the people, can be killed without compunction. At the same time, the fanatic's dealings with those who are not enemy outsiders may remain the same.

Having mentioned Hitler, I suppose it is time for the obligatory discussion of the alleged connection between atheism and some of the twentieth century's mass murderers. The charge that Hitler was an atheist is often made. It is a staple of right-wing religious diatribes against atheism or secular humanism. Hitler's mass murder of Jews and others supposedly shows the consequences of godlessness. Of course, it shows no such thing because, among other reasons, the charge that Hitler was an atheist is false. Those who make this charge are inexcusably ignorant of the relevant facts, have their perceptions distorted by their dogma, and/or are just lying.

Hitler was not an orthodox Christian—in fact, in private he was harshly critical of Christianity—but there is no doubt he believed in God. He invoked God repeatedly, in private and in public, throughout his life. *Mein Kampf* has multiple references to God.[11] (Interestingly, Hitler argued, as do some contemporary believers, that religious faith is necessary for morality.)[12] His speeches are also replete with references to God.[13] Not only did he believe in God, but he also abhorred atheism, which he associated with Communism or, as he called it, Bolshevism. Because National Socialism was a bulwark against Bolshevik atheism, he was confident the Nazis were blessed by God.[14]

But speaking of Communism—what about Stalin, Mao, and the other atheist leaders who carried out mass slaughter? Well, there's no denying they were atheists, but the issue is did their atheism turn them into bad people? Specifically, did their atheism turn them into callous murderers? The cause-effect relationship isn't established here. First, there are at least a few hundred million atheists who are *not* horrible people, so atheism seems unlikely to be the cause of Stalin's or

Mao's indifference to human life. Second, we have a better explanation, namely, the fact that they were ideologues, and their ideology justified the killing of "counterrevolutionaries" and "social parasites." As I just mentioned, religious or ideological fanaticism can motivate people to become mass murderers. In the mind of the fanatic, individual human beings become relatively unimportant compared to the greater glory of God, the protection of the Aryan race, or the achievement of a communist utopia. *It's the dogmatic mind-set that should concern us, whether it's religious dogmatism, racial dogmatism, or political dogmatism.* Mere belief or disbelief in God should not trouble us, whatever our views on the existence of God. There is simply no evidence that one's beliefs about God make one a morally bad person.

Perhaps because of the increasing difficulty of arguing that atheism turns people into scoundrels and miscreants, some believers have tried some different approaches. As I have indicated, there is the argument that atheism, although it may have no perceptible harmful effect on the individual atheist, will eventually lead to societal decay and ruin. I'll discuss that in the next section. But another argument, which applies both to the individual atheist and to society at large, is the contention that while atheists aren't *bad* people, they're not especially *good* people either. Maybe your atheist neighbor won't steal from you, but will she offer to give you a ride to the airport? Are the nonreligious as kind, as altruistic as the religious? And if they are not, isn't that going to negatively affect the well-being of our communities?

Among academic researchers this topic has been the subject of some controversy—much more than the issue of whether the nonreligious engage in harmful actions more frequently than the religious. (The specter of the malevolent atheist is a popular prejudice with essentially no support from social scientists.) Accordingly, it merits some discussion. For those who want a quick answer and can't stand the suspense, the answer is, in general, the nonreligious seem to be as beneficent as the religious, but it's *possible* they may fail to rise to the occasion sometimes for lack of moral reinforcement from others. Let me explain.

The 1975 study on cheating referred to previously also compared the religious and nonreligious in terms of their willingness to perform an altruistic act, namely, volunteering to spend time with some mentally challenged children. The study found no difference between the groups. The conclusion of this study, that there is no link between religious belief and increased frequency of altruistic behavior, has been supported by numerous other studies. On the other hand, there have also been some studies suggesting a link between being religious and altruistic behavior. The literature on this topic is studded with references to, and analysis of the significance of, these apparently inconsistent results.[15]

One problem in analyzing and comparing these conflicting reports is that in many cases we're comparing apples and oranges. The researchers are studying different groups (students in secondary schools, people who attend/don't attend religious services, people who receive solicitations from charities, and so forth), define their research categories differently (e.g., some studies distinguish between those who are "intrinsically" and "extrinsically" religious), and apply different methodologies (self-reports of altruistic conduct, questionnaires about attitudes, observation of conduct during staged situations, and so on).[16] One could be forgiven for us throwing up one's hand and saying there's no solid evidence one way or the other.

However, a recent mammoth study requires attention if for no other reason than it has been taken seriously by many, including a number of scholars, and that is the Faith Matters surveys conducted by Robert Putnam and David Campbell, the results of which were analyzed and published in *American Grace: How Religion Divides and Unites Us*.[17] Putnam and Campbell conclude that their data, taken from nationwide surveys of representative samples of Americans, shows a clear connection between religion and altruism. Not pulling any punches,

Putnam and Campbell expressly assert that "religious Americans are, in fact, more generous neighbors ... than their secular counterparts."[18] However, as the authors clarify, it's not simply being religious that matters, as the connection is *not* between religious belief and altruism, but between involvement in "religiously based social networks" and altruism. Simplifying greatly, involvement in religiously based social networks means attending religious services regularly and hanging out with religious friends. As Putnam and Campbell put it, "it is belonging that matters, not believing."[19] And what does involvement in these religious networks yield? According to Putnam and Campbell, persons involved in such religious networks are more likely to engage in charitable activity or "good deeds," such as volunteering or donating money to a charitable organization, including nonreligious charities, or giving money to a homeless person.

Not unexpectedly, the Putnam/Campbell study has not been universally acclaimed. One significant problem with the study is that it relies on self-reporting of "good deeds." In other words, survey respondents were asked to report to the researchers the acts of benevolence they had performed in the previous twelve months. Therefore, the results may not indicate so much that religiously involved individuals tend to be more altruistic, but rather that for religiously involved individuals it is important for their self-image to be regarded as altruistic. Put another way: the survey may be skewed because there was overreporting of good deeds by the religiously involved.

But reliance on self-reporting is unlikely to explain all of the discrepancy between the frequency of altruistic conduct by the religiously involved and nonreligious Americans. Even if the data is adjusted, there likely would still be some difference. Nonetheless, Putnam/Campbell may be drawing the wrong conclusion, even if we grant that their data is generally reliable.

The Putnam/Campbell study does not establish that nonreligious Americans are less disposed to be altruistic than religious Americans.

Their character may be just as benevolent, generous, or "nice" as religious Americans. What the Putnam/Campbell study may suggest is that because nonreligious Americans do not participate in group activities that remind them of their moral obligations—that trigger their underlying disposition to be altruistic—they engage in fewer altruistic activities than religiously involved Americans.

Moral behavior has been the subject of much study in recent years, by neuroscientists, anthropologists, psychologists, and other researchers. One point of consensus is that we are sometimes motivated by cues or prompts, that is, circumstances in our environment, including ones of which we are not conscious.[20] To borrow some jargon from the literature, our conduct is "primed." A loose, but serviceable definition of "priming" is exposure to some environmental cue that activates associated representations in one's memory, resulting in these representations playing a role, often unconscious, in one's decision making. An example would be seeing brand X detergent in the background of a movie scene, which may incline one to buy brand X the next time one goes shopping. (Hence the importance of product placement in movies.)[21]

As indicated, priming may play a role in moral decision making as well as consumer purchases. It is consistent with the Putnam/Campbell data to infer that those who were involved in religious activities (going to church, getting together with their religious friends) may be reminded—consciously or unconsciously—of their obligation to help others. Certainly, our religious institutions tell us they emphasize to their members the importance of generosity and kindness. Moreover, there is some empirical evidence that church attendance prompts charitable giving (but only on Sundays—that is, the day of attendance).[22]

In the United States, the nonreligious may not experience as many prompts regarding altruism as the religious because they may not belong to groups that remind them of their obligations. There are organizations in the United States that the nonreligious can join, including the Center for Inquiry and the Council for Secular Humanism, two affiliated organizations that have me as their president and CEO. Humanist/atheist organizations do emphasize the importance of ethics, including the value and importance of compassion for others. Unfortunately, our groups are not large—in part because we are not well-known. Less than 0.5 percent of nonreligious Americans belong to a humanist/atheist organization, in some cases because they are not aware there are such organizations.

Being part of a secular civic organization might expose someone to frequent prompts to engage in altruistic activities, but as Putnam/Campbell point out, nonreligious Americans are not as civically engaged as religious Americans.[23] The religious join or participate in the activities of community or civic organizations more than the nonreligious. This may not indicate an unwillingness to be civically engaged on the part of the nonreligious, though. Bear in mind, as discussed earlier in this chapter, many Americans have a very dim view of atheists. Why would you get involved with community organizations if you either had to hide your beliefs or be treated like a pariah? Interestingly, Putnam/Campbell cite the Boy Scouts as one of the community organizations to which the religious belong more often than the nonreligious![24] This result is unsurprising. It's pretty difficult to join an organization that doesn't want you.

Am I exaggerating the extent to which some atheists may be less inclined to engage in civic/charitable activity because of the adverse reactions they might receive? I don't think so. Indeed, a recent incident confirms my point. In December 2013, a young atheist blogger attempted to donate $3,000 to an Illinois library. He was rebuffed, with the librarian saying it would not accept money from someone who belonged to a "hate group."[25] Such rejections hardly provide an incentive to give.

In the final analysis, the Putnam/Campbell study does not show any fundamental difference in religious and nonreligious individuals with respect to their character. Moreover, contrary to the authors' conclusion, their study may not establish that it is religious involvement that fosters a tendency to be more altruistic. Instead, it may be involvement with any group that makes one feel part of a community and, therefore, serves to remind one of obligations toward others.

Some evidence for my interpretation of the Putnam/Campbell data can be found by looking again at the situation in Scandinavia. Denmark and Sweden have large nonreligious populations yet they dispense huge amounts of charitable relief to poor nations; Denmark ranks second, and Sweden third in aid to poor countries.[26] Within their own countries, Danes and Swedes support a wide range of social services. The charitable impulse seems alive and well in Scandinavia. This is speculative, but because lack of religion is not the barrier to social integration in Scandinavia that it is in the United States, the nonreligious may have a greater sense of belonging to their societies in Denmark and Sweden than they do in the United States, and the impulse to act charitably may be reinforced more often by group involvement. In fact, Danes show a high degree of civic involvement, with the typical Dane belonging to over three voluntary associations.[27]

There is one final point of comparison between the conduct of the religious and the nonreligious, and that is with regard to their tolerance of others, especially minority groups or groups whose views or conduct are considered objectionable. The Putnam/Campbell study concluded that religiously observant individuals are significantly more intolerant than the nonreligious. Moreover, "church attendance is strongly associated with lower support for civil liberties."[28] So to put the results of the Putnam/Campbell study in concrete terms: if you are asking for a handout, a religiously involved person might throw you a dollar slightly more often than a nonreligious person. But if you identify yourself as a gay or lesbian when you are asking for help, the religious person may think twice about assisting you, whereas your identity probably will not affect the atheist.

To summarize our discussion about the morality of those who don't believe in God: there is no factual evidence to support the popular prejudice that nonbelievers are less trustworthy and will behave badly more often than the religious. With respect to altruism, there does not appear to be any significant difference in character between religious and nonreligious. There are kind and callous atheists, just as there are kind and callous theists. Admittedly, people who are active in groups that may remind them of their moral obligations may be more generous with their time and money. But this doesn't mean we need to get atheists back in churches, temples, and mosques. Instead, we need to encourage civic engagement by nonbelievers and, in the United States, the first step in that direction is to stop treating atheists like pariahs.

Widespread Atheism and Social Decline

"Can Civilization Survive Without God?" was the sensationalized title given by the Pew Forum on Religion & Public Life to a 2010 conversation/debate between Christopher Hitchens and his brother, Peter Hitchens.[29] That the Pew Forum, a project of the nonpartisan and respected Pew Research Center, would hold a conversation on this topic is by itself revealing. No respectable organization would hold a symposium on the topic "Can Civilization Survive Christianity?" or "Can Civilization Survive Islam?" At least no organization could do so without engendering severe and immediate public criticism. Atheism, though, not only threatens many people, but it is still considered acceptable among some to label it as a threat. Even if it is conceded that the individual atheist may be a good person, there is an abiding concern that the spread of atheism bodes ill for civilization. The spread of atheism is regarded like the spread of the plague—or perhaps the invasion of the body snatchers.

There is no denying the existence of this dread among some believers, however unfounded it may be (and I will discuss why it is unfounded momentarily). In the United States, this anxiety over a tumble into godless anarchy motivates many of those who push for the return of compulsory religious exercises in public schools. Those who advocate for compulsory religious exercises (e.g., teacher-led school prayer) inevitably point to what they see as evidence of moral decline. The evidence of moral decline is debatable to say the least (e.g., access to abortion and same-sex marriage are often included in the parade of horribles), but the sentiment is undoubtedly genuine.

This concern about losing our moral footing as belief in God erodes isn't confined to the United States. Rabbi Jonathan Sacks, an author of a number of books and a life peer in the United Kingdom, has contended in a recent work that morality cannot be sustained in the long run without religion.[30] As with many educated theists, he acknowledges that one does not "have to believe in God to save a drowning child, give food to the hungry, or dedicate your life to fighting poverty in Africa," adding that "[t]he moral sense is prior to the religious sense."[31] Nonetheless, he asserts that over time, if people give up religion "there would be a slow but inevitable breakdown of trust." Sacks explains, "Moralities may be a long time dying but, absent the faith on which they are based, they die."[32]

Sacks's grim prediction is clear, but what is less clear is the basis for this prediction. He makes a number of assertions, but distilled to their essence, they are all variations on the theme that atheists cannot be trusted to do the right thing—absent someone watching them.

There are a couple of peculiar things about Sacks's assertions. First, according to Sacks, theists appear no different than atheists in terms of their core character. Sacks claims that atheists stay in line only because of fear of external surveillance—but then he also says theists stay in line because "God sees. Therefore we are seen."[33] So *both* theists and atheists appear to act appropriately only for prudential reasons. The principal difference between theists and atheists is simply who they think is watching them. One would have thought that some people can be counted on to do the right thing because of their moral character, especially given Sacks's earlier admission that morality precedes religion.

Second, despite his pretentions at high-mindedness, Sack's ultimately relies on a dressed-up version of the timeworn and threadbare myth that atheists cannot be trusted because they do not believe in a God who rewards and punishes. We have already exposed that myth as nothing more than a prejudice. Today's atheists behave as decently as theists. Why should things change just because there may be more atheists in the future? Sacks provides no explanation.

So Sacks doesn't offer us anything other than a big sack of ... rhetoric. But don't let it be said that I have never extended a helping hand to the apologists of religion. I'll supply Sacks and others with something resembling an argument. Here it goes:

"Sure, there are atheists who behave as decently as believers. But that is because we are still in the transition from a culture that is overwhelmingly religious to a secular society. The norms, the virtues that were nourished in our prior religious culture are still present, albeit in increasingly attenuated form, and these influence the behavior of everyone. Put simply, today's nonbelievers are surrounded by believers and their norms, and this has a beneficial effect on their conduct. But the influence of religious culture and religious standards of conduct will fade over time. We're like a family that has inherited a great deal of money, but is not earning any money of its own. The living is easy for now, but the money is going to run out eventually. Without religious faith to renew each generation's commitment to moral values, over time we will devolve into a society of mostly self-centered egotists who will restrain their desires only when they fear others will become aware of their self-interested activity—and perhaps not even then."

The major problem with this argument is that it makes a crucial unwarranted assumption, namely that religion is responsible for our moral norms and our moral behavior. But as Sacks himself concedes, moral behavior is *prior* to religious belief. Granted, religion has been an important vehicle for transmitting and reinforcing moral norms for a long time, but just as morality preexisted religion, there is no persuasive reason for thinking it will not survive religion. Ironically, the one thing that might cause some decline in the observance of moral norms is the constant harping by religious apologists that there's no reason to be moral without God. If this is repeated often enough, for a few people it could be a self-fulfilling prophecy. For most people, however, the foundations of our moral conduct should be little affected either by the decline in religion or by (unsound) arguments that nihilism follows from the rejection of God. The roots of our morality are found in our evolutionary heritage and these roots should not become susceptible to extirpation merely because our beliefs about supernatural beings have changed.

What empirical evidence we have does not lend any support to the claim that morality will not survive the decline of religion. In an effort to find some supporting evidence, Sacks actually feels compelled to discuss ancient history to make his case. After a cursory discussion of the materialist philosophy of Epicurus, who lived from around 341 to 270 BCE, Sacks argues that "[t]he [ancient] Greeks had no concept of the sanctity of life."[34] To say this is painting with a broad brush would be an understatement. First, ancient Greek civilization extended over a long period of time, and attitudes changed, just as they have in the modern era. Second, they may have had different understandings of when killing was wrong, but that they thought killing another human within one's community was presumptively wrong is indisputable: their city-states would have collapsed otherwise. Therefore, to say they had *no* concept of the sanctity of life is just plain wrong. Third, Sacks tries to support his claim by arguing that abortion, infanticide, suicide, and euthanasia were widely accepted by the ancient Greeks. Greek attitudes were much more varied and nuanced than this, as indicated by the Hippocratic Oath and the generally dim view that both Plato and Aristotle had of suicide.[35] Finally, and most importantly, religious belief dominated ancient Greek culture; atheism was rare, being largely confined to a few philosophers and other scholars. Therefore Sacks's attempt to use alleged Greek disdain for the sanctity of life proves nothing. The entire argument is a non sequitur.

Peter Hitchens, in the debate with his brother with which I began this section, offered some examples of contemporary conduct that he suggested showed the harmful effects of declining religious belief. After referencing some horrific murders and other violent acts in the United Kingdom, he then concluded:

> But in fact, this kind of thing is so common at a low level in the grimmer suburbs of English cities that it is actually normal for a lot of people.
>
> This was not the case until quite recently. How has this decline in civilization come about? Well, I think it has come about at least part-ly—and I'm not a single-cause person—but at least partly because there is no longer in the hearts of the English people the restraint of the Christian religion, which used to prevent this sort of behavior.

The principal problem with this argument is that its premises are just false. It's not the case that murder and other forms of violence have increased dramatically in the United Kingdom in comparison with historical levels. Indeed, homicide rates were highest in England, as they were throughout Europe, in the medieval and early modern eras when religious belief was at its zenith.[36]

Although one should be cautious about sweeping generalizations, especially about phenomena such as crime rates that have more than one cause, secularization is correlated with declining levels of violence in several countries. "Murder rates are actually lower in more secular nations and higher in more religious nations where belief in God is deep and widespread."[37] In addition, secularization in many countries is correlated with higher standards of living and strong social safety nets. Thus, one could argue that secularization, far from precipitating a fall into the abyss, makes life better by improving social conditions.

Because widespread rejection of belief in God is a fairly recent phenomenon, with secularization in most countries occurring in just the last few decades, one cannot decisively refute the claim that widespread atheism will lead to social decline. There is insufficient empirical evidence. However, on the other hand, there is nothing to support this conjecture other than prejudice, fear, and the felt need to defend religious belief by any means necessary, including dime-store philosophizing. If it is a question of betting for or against humanity and its ability to survive on its own, without a supernatural net, my money is on humanity.

* * * *

We have examined the alleged connections between God and morality from a number of different angles. In all cases, however, we have found that there is no connection, logical or factual, between God and morality. The independence of morality from religious beliefs supports the arguments set forth in chapters 2 and 3 that religious beliefs have no role to play in public policy debates. The moral implications of our policies can and should be discussed without bringing in religion.

But some have argued that removing religion from our policy discussions is, at best, a pointless exercise. To the extent policy discussions have moral implications, they necessarily are unresolvable. Secular moral reasoning is no better at providing answers than religious moral reasoning. In the next chapter, I will examine the extent to which secular moral reasoning is a practical, not just a theoretical, improvement over religious moral reasoning by considering a contentious public policy dispute, namely the legalization of physician-assisted suicide.

Seven

SECULAR MORAL REASONING
AND PUBLIC POLICY

The Significance of Disagreements about Moral Issues

In the last few chapters, I have addressed some common misperceptions about morality, in particular, the supposed necessary connection between God and morality. One of the reasons some maintain there is this necessary connection is that, according to them, without God as a moral umpire, we will not be able to resolve moral disputes. We will not be able to arrive at the objectively right answer to a moral controversy. We will have unending moral disagreement.

But this viewpoint misunderstands both the extent and significance of disagreement about moral issues. First, as noted, there are certain core moral norms that have been shared by all cultures. These norms and our common sense application of them (for example, recognizing that I can break a promise in order to save a life) help us navigate the vast majority of our interactions with people. In other words, the extent to which there is serious disagreement about moral issues is exaggerated.

Of course, there is no denying that there are areas of moral disagreement. Moreover, arguably, these areas of disagreement have been increasing in number. Our contemporary world is not the world that humans inhabited for most our species' history. Norms that were sufficient for governing behavior within a tribe or clan are not going to be sufficient to resolve definitively the complex issues that arise in a technologically advanced global human community. For example, consider moral disputes relating to organ transplants, in vitro fertilization, and stem cell research. These are among the many issues our ancestors did not have to confront. Even abortion, at least as a reliable, safe method for terminating a pregnancy, is a relatively recent phenomenon in human history. It is not surprising that novel situations produce disagreements about the morality of certain decisions.

These disagreements, though, do not imply that morality is radically subjective. To the contrary, if morality were radically subjective in the sense that moral judgments were merely a statement of personal preference, then there would be *no* disagreements in ethics. If you like chocolate ice cream and I like vanilla, we do not have any genuine disagreement. We just have different preferences. It is not a "mistake" to like vanilla, so there is nothing to dispute.

Most of us do not approach moral disputes as mere matters of taste. We do think that it is possible to be mistaken in one's moral views.

It should be clear that I endorse the position that people can be mistaken in their views on moral issues, which is one reason the secular morality I have been outlining is not "subjective." I have emphasized the importance of secular moral discourse: explaining and justifying one's moral stance in language that is accessible to all. There would be no point to such discourse if my view that abortion is permissible in certain circumstances is equivalent to my preference for vanilla ice cream.

However, we have to be realistic about the limits of moral discourse. With respect to the core norms of the common morality, there is no serious dispute, as we have seen. In part, this is because their connection to the objectives of morality is obvious. With respect to novel, complex moral issues, there may be wide differences of opinion, in part because the connection between differing courses of action to the objectives of morality remains obscure. Consider this question: Is the purchase of a body organ immoral? Why? Will it destabilize the community? Erode trust? Harm cooperative relationships? There may be a sense that it is inherently wrong, but absent some explanation why it is wrong, all we have is an intuition that, by itself, is unlikely to persuade those who hold a different view. But our ability to provide an explanation may be hindered by both the relative novelty of this issue and its distance from the concerns of everyday life. One doesn't need a Ph.D. in ethics, much less a divinity degree, to understand why we should refrain from lying to or stealing from others. Society would collapse were we not able to rely on others to be truthful and respect our property (most of the time). The consequences of a market for body organs are not quite so obvious.

Nonetheless, by reasoning together and reviewing relevant empirical data, we may be able to delineate the consequences of proposed courses of conduct even in novel situations. Once we have an understanding of the consequences, we can discuss, in secular terms, which set of actions is more consistent with our core norms and the objectives of morality. This discussion is unlikely to yield unanimity. Moral disagreement about some issues will not be completely eliminated. However, such a discussion may narrow the range of disagreement. We can rule out certain answers even if we cannot point to one definitive right answer. (In some situations, there may be more than one acceptable answer.) In itself, this is an important achievement. Furthermore, because such a discussion will require participants to specify what they regard as the probable consequences of a course of action and what they find acceptable or unacceptable about such consequences, the discussion will serve to clarify the crux of any disagreement.

So far we have been considering the benefits of secular moral discussions in abstract terms. It is time to look at a specific public policy issue, namely the legalization of physician assistance in dying, to see how a wholly secular policy debate would proceed.

Physician-Assisted Dying for the Terminally Ill

Physician-assisted dying for the terminally ill, also known as physician-assisted suicide, has been the subject of an ongoing public policy debate in many countries, including the United States, for decades now. It is an issue on which the American public remains sharply divided, with about half the population supporting legalization of physician-assisted dying and half opposing.[1] All too frequently, public discussion of the issue does not advance much beyond an exchange of slogans, with "right to die" dueling with "sanctity of life." Furthermore, public discussion, either explicitly or implicitly, often appeals to religious precepts. Perhaps part of the reason for the persisting deep divisions over this issue is precisely that the discussion is often framed in religious terms.

Is it possible to debate this issue in a meaningful way without resort to religious doctrine? Definitely. Indeed, we can have a very robust, productive discussion about this issue without involving religion in any way. There are secular considerations and arguments that can be advanced against legalization, just as there are secular considerations and arguments that support legalization. In the next few pages, I will first describe the circumstances under which most proponents of assisted dying maintain it should be legal and indicate what moral presumptions should apply in these circumstances. I will then sketch some of the key arguments against legalization and address the concerns presented by these arguments. Although I believe an evaluation of these arguments indicates that physician-assisted dying for the terminally ill should be legalized, the point of my discussion is not to persuade the reader to favor legalization. Instead, it is to demonstrate that religious considerations need play no role in the public policy debate.

As a starting point, we should limit our discussion to assisted dying for the terminally ill. At least in the United States, there has been no significant effort to legalize assisted dying on demand or to broaden the class of eligible individuals to include the chronically ill. We should next consider the implications of commonly accepted moral norms relevant to this situation— namely, the norms that we should alleviate suffering and we should respect a person's decisions about matters of great significance pertaining to his/her own body, for example, whether to pursue a course of medical treatment. (Admittedly, this last norm may not be accepted throughout the world.) Like all norms, these create presumptions—presumptions that can be rebutted. There is no absolute requirement to relieve a person's suffering or respect that person's autonomy regardless of the consequences. That said, taken together these norms seem to create a presumption that it is morally permissible to hasten a terminally ill person's death, assuming the person is competent and has made a voluntary request for assistance. There is no more intimate and significant a decision for a person than a decision whether to continue living. When a competent, terminally ill person decides that his/her life is too painful, too degrading, too restricted to be worth living, then the burden shifts to others to show that assistance in dying should not be provided.

If we were considering persons who were not terminally ill, this burden might be fairly easily met. Most persons who want to end their lives are suffering from either temporary or permanent emotional or mental instability. They are often overreacting to a situation that is transient, albeit very emotionally painful. Moreover, persons who are in reasonably good physical condition do not need assistance to end their lives. A request for assistance in dying from a physically healthy, emotionally troubled individual is an attempt to circumvent an important psychological barrier to killing oneself. Generally speaking, if a physically healthy, able-bodied person is too ambivalent to kill himself without assistance, suicide is for him the wrong decision.

But the terminally ill are in a different position. First, unlike persons suffering from transient emotional turmoil, the terminally ill are in an objectively verifiable condition of deteriorating health from which there is no hope of recovery. They are not going to "get over" some emotional setback and go on to lead a long, productive life. Second, unassisted suicide is an option only for those with the physical capacity and means to carry out this act. In the last stages of a terminal illness, most persons lack the ability to hasten their death.[2] They are often frail, with significantly impaired mobility, so violent means are not an option. Furthermore, the state and its licensed agents control access to medications that could bring about a peaceful death. Legally, laypersons cannot obtain barbiturates or similar drugs on their own. A physician must prescribe such a drug and a pharmacist must dispense it. For the terminally ill who wish to hasten their death, a denial of assistance effectively compels them to remain alive against their will. It is not an exaggeration to say that in prohibiting assistance in dying for the terminally ill, the state has appropriated their lives—albeit for a limited period of time. Accordingly, while it may be presumptively immoral in most cases to assist someone to die, in the case of the terminally ill, the presumption goes the other way. In other words, it is presumptively permissible to assist competent terminally ill persons to hasten their deaths.

So far we have been discussing assisted suicide of the terminally ill in general terms, as though any person should be allowed to assist a terminally ill person to hasten his or her death. We should make the discussion more concrete and directly relevant to the public policy debates. Specifically, it is time to consider the significance of *physician* assistance in dying. At least in the United States, debates over legalization have almost always involved legislation that would authorize physician assistance in dying. No state currently authorizes laypersons to provide assistance, nor is there any meaningful effort to have such legislation enacted. Why is that?

There is the obvious reason that only physicians have the authority to prescribe the drugs necessary to bring about a quick, peaceful death, but the reasons go well beyond that. Advocates of physician assistance in dying regard this assistance as part of the continuum of medical care provided by a physician. Physicians, of course, try to restore their patients to health. However, when death becomes inevitable, physicians cannot simply abandon their patients—not without violating their moral obligations as well as their professional commitments. They have an obligation to try to relieve a patient's pain and suffering, consistent with the patient's wishes. In some situations, the patient's physical or mental decline may be intolerable for the patient, due to uncontrollable pain, loss of functions, or inability to interact with loved ones. In these cases—or so some would maintain—a physician's care can include providing a patient with the means to hasten his or her death.

Allowing physicians to consult with their patients openly and candidly about end-of-life care, including assisted dying, has the additional benefit of extending lives. This may seem counterintuitive, but the history of physician-assisted dying in Oregon (where it has been legal since 1997) confirms that many patients who at first express a desire to die instead avail themselves of palliative care options—which they may not have been fully aware of prior to consulting with their physician. Furthermore, roughly one-third of the patients in Oregon who do request medication to hasten their death never utilize these drugs.[3] In other words, they find they are able to withstand the suffering accompanying their condition, in part because they have the assurance they can end their suffering any time it becomes intolerable. Human capacity to endure suffering increases when one has the knowledge that one can end this suffering at any time. In contrast, banning physician assistance in dying precludes candid discussion of some patients' concerns, and pushes some of the terminally ill to make a decision on ending their life while they are still able to do so themselves, resulting in precipitous, uninformed decisions and deaths that are unnecessarily hastened. Some will be motivated by exaggerated fears of the suffering they think they will be compelled to endure, but who can blame them? Perhaps things will not turn out badly, but perhaps they will be trapped inside their bodies for two to three months, immobile, whimpering, waiting for the nurse to notice they need more pain medication. Given that possibility, some will choose to end their life while the gun, the knife, or the noose are still options. In sum, legalizing *physician* assistance in dying can and does result in patients who are better informed about their end-of-life options. Moreover, it can and does encourage some patients to live longer, and it has the effect of causing some of them to forego hastening their death altogether.

Finally, in considering the physician's role, it is important to note that the physician's expertise is crucial in determining whether the patient is competent to make a decision regarding treatment, including treatment that may hasten the patient's death. If a patient lacks decision-making capacity, the moral case for allowing assisted dying is considerably weakened, as there is no presumption that we should respect the stated desires of a person who is incompetent. The jurisdictions that have legalized physician assistance in dying have all enacted procedural safeguards that help ensure the patient is competent to make a decision and that the decision is truly voluntary. For example, in Oregon, the patient must make two oral requests for assistance, at least fifteen days apart, and a written request, and both the patient's treating physician and a consulting physician must confirm that the patient is competent. Furthermore, the treating physician must inform the patient of alternatives to a hastened death, such as hospice care or enhanced pain control, so the patient is made aware of all options when making a decision.[4]

I have now outlined, in secular terms, the parameters of the contemporary debate over assisted dying. The policy issue currently being debated in the United States is whether to legalize physician-assisted dying for the terminally ill pursuant to a statute that contains various procedural safeguards to ensure that the patient requesting assistance is competent and that the patient's decision is both well-informed and voluntary. I have also indicated that given this description of the issue, there is a moral presumption in favor of legalization, given our obligation to reduce suffering and respect the autonomy of others. But this is a presumption only and can be rebutted. So we need to consider whether this presumption is rebutted by secular arguments against legalization.

Arguments Against Legalizing Physician-Assisted Dying for the Terminally Ill

Arguments against legalization can be divided into two sets. One set comprises those arguments that rest on the alleged harmful consequences that would follow legalization. Prior to the legalization of assisted dying in Oregon, and now some other states, such as Washington and Vermont, these arguments were more speculative than empirical, and for that reason, less likely to lend themselves to fruitful debate. Now with a track record from Oregon—and, to a lesser extent, from Washington, where assisted dying became legal in 2009—it is far easier to determine the extent to which these arguments have any force. The other set of arguments is based on the inherent wrongness of killing someone, including oneself. (Opponents of assisted dying almost invariably refer to it as killing.) Here, as the claim is not empirical in nature, debate will have to appeal to reasoning and arguments from coherence. Nonetheless, arguments, and not just unsupported assertions, can still be made.

Those opposed to legalization have generally made four arguments based on alleged harmful consequences. They have argued that post-legalization: (1) the quality of palliative care will decline; (2) various vulnerable segments of the population—the poor, women, minorities—will be adversely affected in disproportionate numbers by the availability of legal assisted dying; (3) assisted dying will not be regulated properly and there will be numerous abuses (for example, some patients being coerced into requesting a hastened death); and (4) assisted dying for the terminally ill will invariably put us on the slippery slope to assisted suicide on demand, nonvoluntary euthanasia, and other dreaded outcomes.[5] If some of these consequences did follow from legalization, they would weigh against the wisdom of legalization. No right is absolute, and although forbidding physician assistance in dying would infringe the autonomy, and prolong the suffering, of some patients, such restrictions might be necessary if they were the only way to avoid significant harm to others. So let's consider these arguments in turn.

Decline in Palliative Care

The fear that legal assisted dying will cause the quality of palliative care to decline is based primarily on the supposition that postlegalization, an attitude of indifference to the terminally ill will become prevalent. If a patient can just "go ahead and die," why expend any efforts on improving, or even maintaining palliative care? This lower quality of palliative care will affect all terminally ill patients, not just those who might be interested in hastening their death. Moreover, the decline in the quality of palliative care postlegalization will pressure some patients into requesting assistance in dying who would not have done so had adequate palliative care been available.

But the evidence from Oregon indicates this fear is unfounded. Not only has the quality of palliative care not declined, but there is evidence that the quality of palliative care has improved.[6] When one considers the dynamics of the debate over physician-assisted suicide, this result should not be surprising. Responsible advocates of physician-assisted dying want improved end-of-life care in general, with the option of assisted dying being only part of the spectrum of care being offered to patients. Accordingly, they want improved palliative care, and have lobbied hard for it. In addition, opponents of assisted dying don't want to see patients opting for a hastened death, so they also have lobbied for improved palliative care, in the hope that this will meet the needs of most patients. The option of physician-assisted dying in no way diminishes the importance of palliative care. To the contrary, it focuses attention on its importance.

Moreover, the supposition that inadequate palliative care may pressure some patients to request assistance in dying has not been supported by the evidence. The record in Oregon establishes that inadequate palliative care is not a significant motivation for requesting assistance in dying. About 90 percent of the Oregon patients who have received assistance in dying were enrolled in hospice, which is widely regarded as the optimum means for providing palliative care.[7]

Disparate Impact on the Vulnerable

With respect to the contention that legal assisted dying will disproportionately affect certain vulnerable populations, one might question whether this is the type of harm that argues against legalization. Upon analysis, this contention rests on the questionable moral premise that the wisdom of legalization depends on whether proportionally more blacks than whites, more women than men, more poor than wealthy, and so on, are pressured into requesting assistance in dying. But what matters is whether persons are being coerced into requesting assistance in dying, *not* the race, sex, or socio-economic background of these persons. Coercing a wealthy white man into requesting assistance in dying is as repugnant as coercing an impoverished African American woman into requesting such assistance.[8]

However, we need not be detained by pondering whether a disparate impact on allegedly vulnerable groups would have moral significance in this context, because there is no evidence whatsoever to indicate there has been a disparate impact. Both in Oregon and Washington, the persons who have requested assistance in dying have been overwhelmingly white, in proportions far exceeding their representation in the general population. Through 2012, exactly one African American patient had requested assistance in dying in Oregon.[9] The vast majority also have been insured and well-educated. The majority also have been men, although not by a large margin—in other words, the male/female ratio is not much different than the male/female ratio in the general population. The fact is the "vulnerable" do not experience any extraordinary risks when physician-assisted dying is legal. Even some of those who are doubtful about the benefits of legalization have conceded that there is no factual support for the disparate impact concern.[10]

The Problem of Abuse

Perhaps the strongest argument against the legalization of physician-assisted dying is that it cannot be effectively regulated and abuses are bound to occur. In particular, there is a concern that terminally ill patients may be manipulated or pressured, directly or indirectly, into requesting assistance in dying. Prior to legalization of assisted dying in Oregon, there were predictions that Oregon would become a suicide mill, with dozens of incidences of abuse each year.

At least in Oregon, these feared consequences have not materialized. There have been no confirmed cases of patients being manipulated or coerced into requesting assistance in dying. Nor is there evidence that patients are being indirectly pressured into requesting assistance because of financial concerns. Information that the state collects regarding patients who received assistance in dying reveals that less than 2 percent have been uninsured and only a little more than 2 percent mentioned financial concerns as a motivation for requesting assistance.[11]

Opponents of legalization have argued that even though there is no hard evidence of abuses, there is anecdotal evidence from a handful of cases suggesting that some patients have been manipulated. For example, in one case, a psychologist who evaluated the patient stated that the patient's daughter had been "somewhat coercive" in urging her mother to avail herself of the option of assisted dying. However, the same psychologist also found the patient capable of making her own decisions.[12]

The inferences to be drawn from the facts in these few cases are disputed. However, this does not prevent us from concluding that to date any abuses have been rare, if they have occurred at all. The question then is whether a few cases of abuse—assuming they have occurred—are sufficient to rebut the presumption that we should allow physician-assisted dying for the terminally ill.

In evaluating the significance of these possible isolated instances of abuse, we should bear in mind that no regulatory scheme is perfect. For example, for safety reasons, we regulate the speed of motor vehicles, but we know both that some speeding drivers will avoid detection and that the current speed limits result in more deaths and serious injuries than would lower speed limits. But no one seriously maintains that we should ban all motor vehicles, and there are few who want more rigorous enforcement of existing speed limits or dramatically lower speed limits. Most of us are willing to accept some injuries and some deaths as the unavoidable cost of vehicular travel at fairly high speeds because there are significant benefits obtained from such travel.

Balancing harms and benefits from legalizing conduct that may expose some to a risk of (unwanted) death is not an exact science—except perhaps for utilitarians, and I am skeptical about the pretentions of this ethical theory. I do not think we can assign an exact number to the instances of abuse that would trigger the conclusion that we should prohibit physician-assisted dying. But given the record in Oregon, we do not have to. Simply because we do not know exactly where to draw the line does not mean there are no situations that do not fall clearly on one side of the line or the other. A few cases of abuse over a sixteen-year history do not imply that legalizing physician-assisted dying is unwise or immoral. The procedural safeguards in place in Oregon (and now in other states) appear to have prevented the level of abuses that would counsel against legalization.

Slippery Slope

Some predicted that once the practice of physician-assisted dying was legalized, the practice would not remain restricted to the terminally ill. Inevitably, assisted dying would be authorized for the chronically ill and then for anyone who wanted it. Nonvoluntary euthanasia—the mercy killing of someone not capable of making his/her desires known—would also become accepted.

Assume for the sake of argument that these would be bad consequences. (Some would dispute this.) There is no indication that Oregon is tumbling down the dreaded slope. There has been no concerted effort to broaden the categories of individuals eligible for assisted dying.

Of course, the slippery slope argument is itself slippery. The proponent of this argument can always maintain that even though the slope is not apparent yet, it will become manifest in the future. However, this argument is speculative at best. One would have to offer a persuasive argument why expansion of the practice of assisted dying to morally dubious cases is unavoidable. That argument has yet to be made.

From the foregoing, it appears that the harmful consequences that some have predicted would follow legalization have not happened. Therefore, the presumption in favor of legalizing physician-assisted dying has not been rebutted.

The foregoing represents a very quick assessment of the arguments based on harmful consequences, and I acknowledge that some may evaluate the arguments differently. That's fine. Again, this is not a brief in favor of physician-assisted dying. Instead, the purpose of this overview has been to show how a meaningful discussion can be carried out without involving religion.

The Inherent Wrongfulness of Physician-Assisted Dying

Much of the opposition to legalizing physician-assisted dying comes from those who maintain that, regardless of any harmful consequences the practice may have on others, it is just wrong. It is an act of killing and killing is always morally wrong (except perhaps in exceptional circumstances, such as cases of self-defense). This position is often maintained by religious organizations and religious individuals. Moreover, it is often maintained by them because of the dictates of their religious beliefs. As I discussed in the closing section of chapter 5, when this position is based on religious precepts, it is usually referred to as the "sanctity-of-life" doctrine.

If this position were always maintained solely on the basis of religious precepts, then it would have no place in a secular policy debate. However, there are those who have adopted and advanced this position without appeal to religious doctrine. For some, it is apparent that what they are doing is reformulating their religious views in secular terms—but that is good. That is what we want religious believers to do. We do not want to exclude the religious from public policy debates. Instead, what we need to insist upon is that positions and arguments be stated in terms accessible to all. That is, they must be stated in secular terms.

The secular argument that physician-assisted dying is intrinsically wrong has as its key premise the claim that intentionally killing a human is always morally wrong. (Sometimes the premise uses the terminology "innocent human" to distinguish cases of self-defense or capital punishment.) It is morally wrong because life is a basic good; life is intrinsically worthwhile. Because intentionally killing a human is wrong, it is wrong for persons to take their own lives, and for others to assist them in doing so.[13]

This position is not implausible. Certainly, we normally consider bringing about another's death to be a bad thing. Death is almost always considered a bad consequence. We take steps to avoid it, and we punish those who intentionally bring about another's death.

Usually, that is. And it is the exceptions that need to be considered because these exceptions may indicate that this argument is not persuasive with respect to the special circumstances of physician-assisted dying.

Moral arguments can be evaluated in several different ways. One way to evaluate an argument is to determine whether its implications are consistent with our settled moral views on similar issues. For example, if we think inflicting pain gratuitously is a bad thing, it is difficult to reconcile that view with the position that we have no moral obligations to nonhuman animals, not even to prevent cruelty.

With respect to the position that hastening a patient's death through physician-assisted dying is wrong, there does seem to be an inconsistency between that position and our accepted practice of allowing patients to hasten their deaths by stopping medical treatment. In almost all developed countries, it is now established that patients have a right to stop treatment even when it is known that doing so will very likely result in their death. Moreover, when the patient is incompetent, this right may be exercised by a surrogate, such as a spouse or parent. This practice, sometimes called "passive euthanasia," is no longer a subject of legal controversy in many countries, including the United States, nor, for most people, is it a subject of moral controversy. So if a physician can hasten a patient's death by removing a ventilator, why cannot a physician assist in hastening a patient's death by prescribing a lethal dose of medication?

A standard response at this stage of the discussion is to draw a distinction between "killing" and "letting die." Prescribing a lethal dose of medication is, allegedly, killing the patient; withdrawing life support is letting die.

Although this distinction has been invoked by many, including the U.S. Supreme Court, it does not withstand moral analysis.[14] In both cases, the physician performs an action that is part of a causal chain that may result in death. Removing a ventilator is as much of an action as writing a prescription. Furthermore, this distinction focuses on morally irrelevant factors. What is critical in both the situation involving withdrawal of treatment and the situation in which the physician prescribes a lethal dose of medication is the patient's authorization of the act. A physician who removes life support without proper authorization is, arguably, murdering the patient. Certainly, the physician would be subject to both moral condemnation and legal prosecution. So it is not the dependence of the patient on life support that allows the action to escape moral condemnation; instead, it is the patient's authorization. But in physician-assisted dying, it is the patient who authorizes the act as well. (Indeed, in the states that permit physician-assisted dying, surrogates cannot make the decision on behalf of the patient, so there is less chance that the patient's wishes are being disregarded than in the cases involving withdrawal of treatment, where surrogates often give the authorization.)

Another distinction sometimes offered is that in a situation involving withdrawal of treatment, the physician does not intend the patient's death.[15] Instead, the physician merely intends to relieve the patient's suffering by removing unwanted, burdensome treatment. In considering this distinction, one should first ask whether intentions are capable of such tidy segregation. In particular, is there always a clear distinction between an intent to end suffering and an intent to end life? Second, and more important, a similar distinction can be made in those cases where a physician prescribes a lethal dose of medication. At least arguably, what the physician intends to do is not to end the patient's life, but rather to provide the patient with an option—an option that helps the patient deal with his distressing situation. The physician does not intend the patient's death, which is something that may or may not happen through use of the prescribed medication. As already indicated, roughly one-third of the patients in Oregon who receive the prescription from their physician never ingest the fatal drug. Under these circumstances, in which the physician's actions are actually *less* likely to result in a patient's death than the withdrawal of life-sustaining treatment, it is difficult to see why the physician must be regarded as having intended the patient's death whereas the physician who withdraws life support is not regarded as having intended the patient's death.

The foregoing indicates that there is some tension, if not outright inconsistency, between the view that it is permissible to withdraw life-sustaining treatment and the view that physician-assisted dying is inherently immoral. But we should not leave the argument there. First, some may take the position that withdrawal of life-sustaining treatment is wrong, thereby removing the inconsistency while maintaining the condemnation of physician-assisted dying. In fact, although this is a minority view now, there are some people who take this position, including a number of Catholics.

More important, any time we are presented with a moral rule that seems intuitively plausible yet also seems overly broad as applied to certain special circumstances, we should dig deep and try to discern the underlying rationale for the rule. When we have a proper understanding of the purposes of the rule, we may have a better sense of the scope of its application.

What are the secular reasons for condemning and prohibiting killing? This may strike some as a silly question, but if morality is not merely a set of instinctive reactions or rules that we are supposed to follow blindly, we should always be able to describe the objectives we hope to achieve by implementing and following a moral rule. The prohibition of killing is common to all cultures and a moment's reflection suffices to show why. People want to live. They have an interest in living, and killing them harms those interests. Moreover, because this strong desire to live is shared by almost everyone, killing not only harms the individual, but it also harms the community by making it impossible for the community to live together in peace. No society could function without a prohibition on killing.

This rationale serves to explain why we prohibit killing and are justified in doing so in almost all circumstances. But this rationale may not apply in a situation where a competent person is terminally ill, is suffering, and has expressed a firm desire to hasten his death. In these exceptional circumstances, the individual's interests are not being harmed nor is there any threat to the peace of the community if a physician assists him in hastening his death. Allowing death to be hastened in these circumstances does not serve as a precedent for allowing the killing of people against their will or even the consensual killing of physically healthy individuals. We can maintain the general prohibition on killing while at the same time acknowledging that physician-assisted dying for the terminally ill is morally permissible.

Summary of the Discussion

Lengthy books have been written on the subject of assisted dying or assisted suicide, and each of the arguments and counterarguments sketched here can easily be amplified. My aim has not been to provide a comprehensive or definitive set of arguments on this public policy issue. Instead, I wanted to illustrate how arguments for and against the legalization of physician-assisted suicide can be made entirely in secular terms, without any reference to religious doctrine. I invite the reader to look over the arguments once again. Would invoking religious doctrine add anything of substance to these arguments? I don't think so. What a religious argument would do is provide its proponents with a false sense of certainty while simultaneously shutting down any meaningful discussion. That way lies impasse and confrontation. Not only is religion not needed in policy discussions, but use of religious doctrine inhibits productive discussion.

The example I have used to illustrate this point is the debate over legalization of physician-assisted dying for the terminally ill. But there is nothing special about this issue that makes it more appropriate for a discussion conducted entirely in secular terms. We could similarly conduct debates on same-sex marriage, abortion, stem cell research, climate change policy, tax rates, and other contentious issues entirely in secular terms. Furthermore, if we are to engage each other productively, we must do so.

Because too many have been accustomed to relying on religious doctrine in policy discussions, it is appropriate to close this chapter with a brief discussion of method when approaching policy issues with a moral dimension.

The first step seems obvious, but nonetheless is often overlooked. One must first define the issue under consideration with some precision. If the issue is physician-assisted dying for the terminally ill, do not confuse this with assisted dying for anyone who wants it. Second, using the norms of the common morality, one should try to discern what moral presumptions may be relevant to the discussion. For example, in the debate over same-sex marriage, there is arguably a presumption, derived from the principle of respect for autonomy, that same-sex couples should be able to enter into long-term relationships, and these relationships should receive the same legal recognition and benefits as the long-term relationships entered into by heterosexual couples. Next, one should consider the implications of a particular policy position. Would recognition of same-sex marriage undermine respect for marriage as an institution? Would it lead to the recognition of polygamous marriages? One must also consider how one's position coheres with settled moral principles. One such principle relevant to the same-sex marriage debate may be that the state has a limited interest in regulating private relationships. Finally, one needs to try to discern the underlying rationale for the principles one advocates. If someone is opposed to same-sex marriage because it has traditionally been rejected, was that rejection based on some experience with the instability of same-sex relationships or society's general condemnation of same-sex relationships on the ground that they are "unnatural"? And if the belief in the deviancy of same-sex relationships is now widely regarded as having been based on an erroneous understanding of human sexuality, has the rationale for reliance on tradition been undermined?

Application of this method will not yield unanimous agreement or point us unmistakably in the direction of the one right answer to a moral dispute. As I have mentioned, in some cases there may not be one right answer. However, this method will assist us in our discussions with each other as we try in good faith to resolve some of our differences. Secular policy debates seldom yield certainty—and that is a good thing. If we are to live together in peace, we need to live with ambiguity and an awareness of our own fallibility. We need to respect each other and listen to each other, and secularism provides the best means for accomplishing these objectives.

Eight

LIVING TOGETHER

The principal aim of this book has been to show the necessity of secularism. For democratic discourse to be successful, we must reason together in terms everyone can understand. Among other things, this means religious doctrines cannot be invoked as justifications for public policy. This is true even for public policies that have moral implications. The last few chapters have demonstrated that we can discuss moral issues without use of religious precepts. Indeed, in a religiously pluralistic society, this is the only practical way to discuss moral issues. To understand each other, to engage each other, we need to use a common language and that is the language of secularism.

As I have emphasized at various points, secularism is not the same as atheism. It's perfectly consistent for someone to be religious and also to be committed to secularism. Indeed, millions of people in Europe, North America, and elsewhere already are religious secularists. And because my concern has been to argue for secularism, not atheism, this book is devoid of arguments against the existence of God. I have criticized various religious beliefs, but with the goal of showing why we can't rely on these beliefs to guide us on issues of morality and public policy.

Of course, there will be those, both religious and nonreligious, who will find my approach troubling or unsatisfactory. I anticipate many religious will regard my approach with deep misgivings and reservations. To begin, I am an atheist and for some that may be sufficient grounds for suspicion. Moreover, in arguing that we can have morality without God, am I not marginalizing God, perhaps to the point of insignificance? An insignificant God hardly seems much of an improvement over a nonexistent God.

On the other hand, I anticipate many atheists will protest vehemently that I've been too soft on religion. To use the term often hurled by atheists at other atheists who are considered insufficiently critical of religion, I may be accused of being an "accommodationist." Why pull my punches? Humanity would be better off without religion, period. Why not argue against religious beliefs comprehensively, instead of merely trying to separate religion from morality and public policy?

This chapter will address both of these concerns. I will then turn to a discussion of how to reconcile religiously motivated claims of conscientious objection with the principles of secularism. I will end with a sketch of a vision for a flourishing secular society.

Reasoning Together: The Religious Perspective

It may seem inappropriate if not unseemly or arrogant for me, an atheist, to explain why someone can remain religious while also being committed to secularism, but, to begin, how people interpret the implications of their religious beliefs is a matter of concern for all of us. (Just as how people interpret the implications of atheism is a concern for all of us.) Second, having been a believer into my young adulthood, I know something about religion and the role it plays in a believer's life. Finally, and most importantly, whether an argument is sound, whether it makes sense is something that is not dependent on the identity of the person making the argument. Either what I say here rings true or it doesn't.

That in the past, God has been understood as playing an important role in morality is an understatement. As discussed in previous chapters, God has been seen as having multiple morality-related roles, such as lawgiver, enforcer, guarantor of objectivity. That said, it's an impoverished understanding of God that views God as having no significance apart from undergirding the institution of morality.

Religion is a complex phenomenon, which is why it's difficult to isolate one cause or even several causes for religious belief. Similarly, religion plays a complex role in the lives of many people. Some find in religion a source of community. Religion can also be a source of courage in the face of tragedy or some of the inevitable heartaches that accompany human existence. Religion is also regarded as a means of being in harmony with the order of the universe. Still others find in religion what they would describe as a point of contact with the transcendent ground for our being, something that satisfies their spiritual yearning. It provides meaning to their lives. In addition, religion brings to many a sense of peace and tranquility. Finally, even religious secularists—those who recognize that the content of morality is for humans to determine—may find inspiration to act morally through their belief in God. Religion can play all these roles, and does play some or all of these roles in the lives of religious secularists, without God also being a moral dictator, adviser, umpire, or enforcer.

The noted theologian Harvey Cox made a similar point some decades ago in his classic work, *The Secular City*. A secularized world does not mean the death of God or the end of religion. People can recognize their responsibility for making and justifying moral decisions without relinquishing belief in God. As Cox stated, "There is no reason that man must believe the ethical standards he lives by came down from heaven inscribed on golden tablets. ... Secularization places the responsibility for the forging of human values, like the fashioning of political systems, in man's own hands."[1]

Let me go further and argue that any deity worth our admiration is not a deity that would want us to be forever dependent on his commands. If our existence and our nature can be traced in some way to the actions of a loving, transcendent being, then that being presumably wants us to use the reason and autonomy we possess. God wants us to reason with our fellow humans about morality and public policy, not to be mindlessly obedient to his directives.

The metaphor most often used to describe God is that of a loving parent. If that metaphor has any element of truth in it, then God would not want to control our lives through his commands. Parents do not want to rule the lives of their children forever. They want them to mature, to take responsibility for themselves. One of the greatest joys a parent has (it certainly was for me) is to see one's children become fully functioning adults, able to come to their own decisions and to justify these decisions. Requiring one's children to adhere to one's dictates after they have chronologically moved beyond childhood is to infantilize them.

Almost all, if not all, early humans did believe in deities who served as unseen enforcers of the group's norms. There may have been some cultural advantage to such beliefs, as these beliefs may have increased group solidarity and collaboration at a time when humans were just developing the notions of moral rules and codes of conduct.[2] Religious beliefs and ceremonies also served as useful means of transmitting and inculcating social and moral norms. These links between religious beliefs and morality have persisted for much of human history, but the connections, though arguably useful at one time, are not necessary. Moreover, in a global human community with religiously diverse beliefs, tying morality to religion produces more harm than benefit. What may have been useful, or at least relatively benign, for early humans doesn't serve us well today.

Secularism doesn't entail a rejection of God, but it does implicitly recognize that the relationship between the believer and God has changed. It has matured. Humanity has lived in God's basement long enough. It is time for humanity to move out, become independent, and get its own apartment.

Reasoning Together: The Atheist Perspective

We atheists reject belief in God (and gods in general). Atheists maintain there is insufficient evidence to support such a belief. Depending on one's description of God, the existence of such a being ranges from unlikely to logically impossible. So theists are mistaken in claiming there is a deity. Given the proper occasion, for example, when someone argues in a book, speech, or conversation that God exists, atheists can and should oppose that claim by appropriate means. No belief should be off-limits from critical examination, and it is neither ill-mannered nor offensive to dispute the claims made by those who are religious. Truth is an important value, for theist and atheist alike, and we show no respect for theists when we stay silent in the face of their claims. Indeed, if we stay silent we are implicitly conveying the message they are so immature or emotionally vulnerable that they "can't handle the truth." Plain speaking is a virtue; it's the best way to show we regard our interlocutor as our peer. (For these reasons, among others, I do not regard myself as an "acommodationist.")

However, all that being said, should we nonreligious make a concerted effort to persuade the religious to give up their beliefs? I don't think so. Here's why.

Yes, we atheists maintain that theists are mistaken. But so what? So what if the religious hold false beliefs? Does that fact by itself make any material difference to us? All of us are mistaken about something, including facts that may not be unimportant, such as the identity of our congressional representatives, the implications of Einsteinian relativity, and the location of the Panama Canal. But most such mistakes result in no more than mild consternation or amusement depending on the situation, and we're not terribly troubled by the fact that we humans hold false beliefs in a number of different areas. We accept our fallibility.

Of course, the false beliefs of others *do* become our concern when these beliefs cause us harm. So the real issue is: does someone's belief in God cause others harm?

Let's first consider the harm that might result from day-to-day dealings with others. It seems to me indisputable that, by itself, belief in God does not make one a better person or worse person, just as disbelief in God does not make one a better person or worse person. As I have already discussed, in terms of their routine interaction with others, there is little to distinguish the religious from the nonreligious. One's metaphysics is simply not a reliable predictor of one's moral character. Nor, for that matter, is one's professed ethics a reliable predictor of one's true moral character. Examples abound of clergy who preach love, honesty, and kindness, but turn out to be frauds and predators. On the other hand, some of the biggest hypocrites I have known are atheists who speak and write eloquently about the importance of moral values, but in their dealings with others have shown themselves to be duplicitous, egotistical, self-aggrandizing, and corrupt. We will have liars, cheats, thieves, and scoundrels with us until the end of the human race, regardless of our religious beliefs. Accordingly, improvements in personal morality cannot be a reason for persuading the religious that their beliefs are in error.

When religious beliefs can cause harm is when they motivate believers to seek to impose their views on others or when these beliefs shape their views on public policy. Many of the religious have sought and continue to seek to impose their beliefs by enlisting the support of the government. This support can range from laws prohibiting individuals from abandoning their religion or criticizing it (such as the laws forbidding apostasy and blasphemy in some Islamic countries) to laws that passively support religion by allowing religious symbols to be displayed on public property. Whatever form government support for religion takes, it is wrong. It is a violation of freedom of conscience. Everyone should be free to come to their own conclusions about the existence of the supernatural without compulsion, prodding, or oversight by the state.

But notice that although religious beliefs surely motivate some of the religious to use the government as a crutch for their beliefs, other individuals who are religious are staunch defenders of church-state separation. Indeed, as we have seen (chapter 2), in the United States, the individuals responsible for providing us with constitutional guarantees of religious freedom were probably all theists, to some degree (although some, such as Jefferson, were tepid deists). In other words, it's possible for a person to be religious and also support a secular government. So if we are concerned about combating preferential treatment for religion, it's not necessary to persuade the religious to become atheists; we only need to persuade most of them of the justice and advantages of a secular state. Many in the developed world are persuaded already.

This leaves public policy. Undoubtedly, religious beliefs have had a harmful effect on public policy, not just because of the specific policies that some believers feel compelled to support—whether it's prohibiting stem cell research or teaching creationism in public schools, as in the United States, or denial of equal educational and employment opportunities to women, as in many parts of the Islamic world—but also because of their pernicious effects on democratic discourse. As I have pointed out at length, the only way we can reason together effectively is by acknowledging the necessity of secularism. We cannot use religious dogma as a justification for public policy; we must base public policy on secular concerns and empirical evidence.

Here again, though, many religious people already acknowledge the necessity of secularism. As to the rest—buy them a copy of this book! In all seriousness, although we have reason to be concerned about religious influence on public policy, removing this influence does not require the removal of religious belief. It is not religious belief in and of itself that is of concern, but the mind-set of all too many of the religious that their doctrines should be reflected in the laws and regulations that govern us all, and, furthermore that they need not provide any justification for their support for a particular public policy other than "God says so." If we are to have a truly democratic society, we need most of the people to break free of this mind-set.

Here some of my fellow atheists may object that we cannot hope to persuade a sufficient number of the religious to break free of this mind-set until we persuade many more people to give up their religious beliefs. Admittedly, for some individuals their religious beliefs so pervade their thinking and their life that they cannot conceive of reasoning about ethics and policy matters in secular terms until they stop believing in God. What percentage of religious believers have this level of commitment to their beliefs is difficult to determine, but it seems safe to say that in the developed world, it's probably no more than a slim majority or a substantial minority of the religious. A recent survey in the United States reveals that about 45 percent of Americans believe political leaders should rely on their religious beliefs when making political decisions, whereas 53 of Americans think they should not rely on their religious beliefs.[3] But of the 45 percent who believe religion should influence the decisions of politicians, well over half think religious beliefs should only "somewhat" influence politicians. These "somewhats" are the persons who, I believe, could be persuaded of the benefits of secularism even if they remain religious. And if they were so persuaded, then there probably would be a sufficient number of Americans to make the United States not only a secular state but a secular society.

Yes, of course there will remain religious individuals who will resist secularism and reject any and all arguments advocating secularism. But what's the alternative? To try to persuade them to give up religion entirely by a frontal assault on their beliefs? Sure, that strategy can work for some, but bear in mind that the religious believers who adamantly reject secularism are precisely the ones most difficult to reason with, so the odds of persuading them that their religious beliefs are unfounded are low.

In sum, if religion were purely a personal matter, the religious beliefs of others would be of little concern to us. It's when the religious try to impose their beliefs on us or use their beliefs to shape public policy that religion becomes an object of serious and legitimate concern. But to eliminate that harm, we need not eliminate religion, we need only convince the religious of the wisdom of secularism. We want the religious to reason together with us about issues of common concern using the common language of secularism. If they do that, does it really matter to us atheists that they believe in a deity?

The Issue of Religious Exemptions from Legal Obligations

In recent decades, there have been increasing efforts to carve out religious exemptions from legal obligations that apply to everyone, or, as lawyers phrase the issue, exemptions from neutral laws of general applicability. In the United States, for example, these efforts have resulted in the enactment of the Religious Freedom Restoration Act (RFRA) and the Religious Land Use and Institutionalized Persons Act (RLUIPA).[4] RFRA provides that if a law burdens a religious belief or practice, the government must show that the law serves a compelling government interest in the least restrictive way; otherwise, the government must grant an exemption to the religious objector. RLUIPA mandates a similar test in the context of land use controversies and prisoners' rights disputes.

An entire book could be devoted to the troublesome issue of legal exemptions for religious beliefs.[5] Here, I limit myself to indicating that the grant of religious exemptions can, but need not be, inconsistent with secularism.

Depending on how broadly laws such as RFRA and RLUIPA are interpreted, religious exemptions could fracture the unity of the secular state. Instead of one law for all, we would have a situation where supposedly "general" laws would be riddled with various exemptions for adherents of different religious beliefs. For example, in a law regulating the provision of health care, we might have several different exemptions for Catholics, Muslims, Jehovah's Witnesses, Scientologists, and Christian Scientists, all of whom may have objections to some generally accepted medical practice or procedure.

However, exemptions based on conscientious objection to general laws need not run afoul of the principles of secularism, if certain conditions are met. The first condition is indicated by the phrasing of this paragraph's lead sentence. It is *conscientious* objection, not merely religiously based objections, that should be permitted to provide a basis for an exemption from a law of general applicability. The nonreligious have moral scruples too, and it improperly privileges religious beliefs to regard only religious objections as entitling one to a legal exemption. In a secular society, there is no principled basis for treating religious objections to a law differently than objections grounded in a nonreligious person's moral norms.

The manner in which the United States interpreted the draft law during the Vietnam War effectively recognized that secular moral convictions are entitled to as much weight as religious objections. In *Welsh v. United States*,[6] the Court interpreted the conscientious objector provision of the Universal Military Training and Service Act, which exempted from combatant service anyone who by "religious training and belief" objected to participation in war. The *Welsh* Court interpreted the term "religious" very broadly to include any ethical or moral belief held with "the strength of traditional religious convictions."[7] Any other result would have violated the Establishment Clause, as the concurrence of Justice Harlan acknowledged. [8]

The other condition for making exemptions for conscientious objection consistent with secularism is to allow such exemptions only when the law directly compels a person to undertake or refrain from undertaking a certain action and the exemption will not unduly burden others. In other words, the exemption relates to self-regarding behavior. Easy cases would allow religious holidays and religious garb for students and the provision of meals free of taboo foods to prisoners. In most circumstances, such exemptions burden no one, as no significant secular purpose is served by forcing a student to wear "immodest" clothing or a Muslim inmate to eat pork.

Exemptions from combatant service may seem to violate the requirement that others not be unduly burdened, but in this case the burden of military service is imposed by the government, not by the person seeking the exemption, and it is doubtful that excusing a few thousand individuals from combat roles will place the combatants at any greater risk than they are already. (Granted, it might be a different situation if there were millions of conscientious objectors.). Moreover, under United States law, the conscientious objector was not relieved of his obligation to serve. Instead, the objector was assigned to alternative service, either a noncombatant role or civilian service. Thus, in some way the national interest was served. Finally, in the military situation, there is the pragmatic consideration that it is pointless to train and arm a person who will refuse to fight. Placing a conscientious objector in a foxhole will burden his fellow soldiers more than allowing him to serve the country in some other capacity.

The circumstances under which exemptions become questionable are situations where the objector is effectively trying to govern the actions of others. In recent years, there have been a number of cases where health care workers have objected to medications or procedures being utilized by others. For example, pharmacists have objected to providing some forms of contraception, and have even refused to transfer prescriptions for these medications, while also maintaining they should receive no discipline from their employer for these actions. Interference with the choices and actions of others is an illegitimate and impermissible use of the concept of conscientious objection. Allowing pharmacists to refuse to provide services when they object to others' health care decisions would be analogous to not only allowing female Muslim students to wear a hijab, but also forcing all other female students to wear hijabs because of the offense they would otherwise give to the Muslim students.

My aim here is not to catalog the legitimate and illegitimate claims of conscientious objection. Rather, I am pointing out that recognition of claims of conscientious objection is not necessarily inconsistent with secularism provided it does not privilege religious beliefs over secular moral claims and exemptions are limited to truly self-regarding conduct. Any discussion of the consequences of granting a particular exemption must, of course, involve secular considerations only.

Flourishing Together

The foregoing sections show how the religious and the nonreligious can reason together and live together. Sure, there will be tensions and disputes, but if we commit to the principles of secularism, then our differences should not lead to violence or the fracturing of society along religious lines.

But it's one thing to have a functioning society; it's another to have a flourishing society. It's one thing to understand the necessity of cooperation; it's another to have the desire to help others. We want the religious and nonreligious to tolerate each other, but we should also want mutual respect between religious and nonreligious. Collaboration that is grudging is not likely to be as effective or rewarding as collaboration that is motivated by a genuine desire to work together.

Some may think that to foster this respect, we must refrain from criticizing each other's beliefs. As I have already indicated, I do not think that is the case. Persons who make claims should be prepared to defend them, and it is no sign of disrespect to disagree with someone's claims. Here let me make brief reference to the controversy surrounding the so-called New Atheists, exemplified by writers such as

Richard Dawkins, Sam Harris, Dan Dennett, and the late Christopher Hitchens. These individuals have been vigorous in their criticism of religious beliefs, which in turn has subjected them to criticism for being intolerant, arrogant, and mean-spirited. It is not my task to defend everything these individuals may have stated; among other reasons, I do not keep track of everything they say. However, in general, criticism of them has been unwarranted. They have provided a valuable service in breaking a taboo. No claim, religious or otherwise, should be immune from criticism, and those who assert claims with the goal of persuading others have no cause to be offended by those who present objections to those claims. Many religious feel compelled to spread the "good news." Fine. But they can't complain if some find their message neither reliable news nor especially good.

But we can and must distinguish beliefs from the person who holds them. There are boundaries that should not be crossed if we are to foster respect for each other. The easiest line to identify (if not always to observe) is the line dividing criticism of an argument from attacks on the person. We should refrain from personal insult. Calling someone stupid or evil because of their beliefs about God accomplishes nothing and is unjustified.

Other limits relate to context. Not every reference to God is the assertion of a claim or an invitation to a discussion. "God bless you!" does not require a rebuttal. Similarly, it does not serve any useful purpose to yell out at someone's religious memorial service that "God and the afterlife are just childish delusions!" This would be the secular analogue of the absurd and obnoxious funeral protests by the members of the Westboro Baptist Church.

Let me suggest one other area where comments about another person's beliefs are at best pointless, and at times are little better than condescending put-downs. I'm referring to remarks about "meaning," and the relationship between God and a meaningful life. Remarks of this type may not seem to be uncivil because they are often made in the guise of a reasoned argument, accompanied by references to various works of literature or philosophy, but they lack any real substance and are just a subtle way of denigrating someone else's beliefs. It's a commonplace among many of the religious that only God can make our lives meaningful. It is not just the ordinary believer who makes this claim; it is a staple of religious scholars, perhaps because they think this claim is less susceptible to rebuttal than some of the standard arguments for God.

Of course, the implication of the contention that life without God would be meaningless is that atheists have meaningless lives. Occasionally, this implication is left hanging, demurely unstated—but typically the theist is eager to drive home the point. For example, John Haught, a theologian at Georgetown University, does not shrink from drawing this inference. To the contrary, he enthusiastically endorses this implication. Indeed, one of his complaints about the New Atheists is that they do not understand the significance of their atheism. In a revealing interview in *Salon*, Haught stated that the New Atheists are philosophically and theologically unsophisticated because they think they can drop "God like Santa Claus, and [keep] going on with the same old values." Haught prefers Nietzsche and existentialist thinkers such as Sartre and Camus who would "think out the implications of a complete absence of deity. . . . The implications should be nihilism."[9]

Nietzsche and the tired school of existentialist philosophers remain the perennial favorites of theologians—despite their negligible influence on contemporary philosophy—because with their angst and their hand-wringing over the alleged absurdity of life, they're poster children for the theologians. Their observations about the alleged absurdity of life mirror the theologians' claims about the importance of God. God, the theologians claim, provides the transcendental justification for meaning, for hope. Sartre and Camus implicitly accepted this claim; they just rejected belief in God. It is no surprise, therefore, that they concluded that without God, life is absurd.

This conclusion should be resisted, however. Existentialism produced some good literature—and a lot of bad philosophy. The weighty claim that we need God to give meaning to our lives and that nihilism is the unavoidable consequence of a godless universe cries out for a compelling argument. But no such argument has ever been advanced. Instead of a compelling argument, we get bald assertions, supported by nothing beyond empty rhetoric, a smug sense of certainty, and a conviction that if one repeats this claim often enough it must be true.

When one analyzes the claim that we need God—something that lies beyond our lives—to give meaning to our lives, one sees the resemblance of this claim to the claim that we need God—something that lies beyond our lives—to ground morality. And the claim that God is essential for meaning suffers from some of the same deficiencies as the claim that God is needed to ground morality. We have seen how morality does not need a "gold standard," that is, something outside of the institution of morality, to be pragmatically justified. Morality serves human needs and interests, and its justification is found *within* human experience. Likewise, there is no need to look beyond our own lives for our lives to possess meaning. The theist is effectively claiming that meaning and purpose need to be forced upon you from the outside; they are imposed by God. To the contrary, the atheist maintains that we can find our own meaning and purpose *within* our experience. Meaning and purpose can't be forced on you. If a person is to find meaning, it must be forged by that person herself. One gives one's life meaning by asserting one's autonomy and using that autonomy to give shape and direction to one's life. An atheist doesn't leave fulfillment in life in a deity's hands; he sets out to achieve it. Where Haught sees nihilism, I see responsibility.

"But our lives are short, sometimes tragically so, and all our beloved projects and relationships are ultimately doomed to irrelevancy, and, therefore, meaninglessness." Yes, our lives are finite, but why should we accept the proposition that our lives must last forever to have real value? As Bertrand Russell noted, "Happiness is nonetheless true happiness because it must come to an end, nor do thought and love lose their value because they are not everlasting."[10] The religious tell us that life is a good thing, and this a view I share. I would only add that there is no reason it can't be good even though it is transitory. Indeed, one can argue it is precisely because our lives are finite that we properly regard them as valuable. That smile, that kiss, our child's first words—all the moments we treasure have genuine value because they are irreplaceable and intrinsically worthwhile, not doomed to be reduced to insignificance by an eternal existence elsewhere that many religious assure us is our *real* destiny.

Here we see the atheist, should he or she be so inclined, can turn the tables on the theist and argue that the existence of God, far from investing our lives with meaning, would actually drain any significance from our lives. After all, what are we but cogs in God's great cosmic machine, servants to a plan of which we remain largely ignorant and over which we have zero control? *That* is supposed to give our life meaning?

But I would urge atheists to resist that temptation (except where necessary to deflect the religious missionary). Arguments about what really gives life meaning are no less condescending when they emanate from the atheist than when they emanate from the theist. In fact, the atheist has less excuse for making such an argument. We atheists should recognize that the significance humans find in life is not going to be the same for everyone and is going to reflect our different outlooks, perspectives, and worldviews. Religious persons will continue to think that their relationship with God is very significant and does lend meaning to their lives regardless of what atheists say. Both the religious and nonreligious would do well to invest their time and energies in matters other than disputes about what gives life meaning.

Perhaps that will be the indicator that we have arrived at the point of authentic respect for one another: when we cease trying to persuade each other who has a more meaningful life and instead try to harness our shared strength into making the world a better place for all of us. We can do this. We can do this if we put our personal religious beliefs aside and speak to each other in the common language of secularism.

ACKNOWLEDGMENTS

Drafts of the introduction and chapter one were read by Russell Blackford, Tom Flynn, Stephen Law, and Anne Lindsay; Russell and Stephen helped me brainstorm the title for the book.

Tim Binga, Director of Libraries for the Center for Inquiry, provided research assistance, especially in connection with chapter two.

The board of directors for the Center for Inquiry provided me with an unpaid leave of absence in 2013, which enabled me to research and write a substantial portion of the book. I am grateful for this consideration.

I thank the publishers who provided permission to incorporate passages from some of my previously published works, in modified form, in this book.

I am very grateful to Kurt Volkan, publisher at Pitchstone Publishing, for his encouragement of this work and for shepherding this work skillfully and expeditiously through the editing process.

One benefit of my position as president & CEO of the Center for Inquiry is that I am in frequent contact with the supporters of the Center for Inquiry, including many people who are scholars or writers. I have profited considerably from conversations I have had with such individuals through the years, and this book reflects, in part, ideas and arguments which grew out of these conversations. Many thanks to all those who have shared their thoughts with me.

Other than the brief leave of absence the board of directors graciously provided me, this work was written at nights and weekends, sandwiched in between my work obligations. My love and gratitude to Debra for her patience and understanding.

NOTES

Chapter 1: An Unprecedented Moment in Human History

1. Phil Zuckerman, *Society Without God* (New York: New York University Press, 2008).

2. Phil Zuckerman, "Atheism: Contemporary Numbers and Patterns," in *The Cambridge Companion to Atheism*, ed. Michael Martin (New York: Cambridge University Press, 2007), pp. 47–65. Exact measures of nonbelief are difficult to achieve because of methodological hurdles, as Zuckerman notes. A 2012 worldwide survey confirmed an increase in the number of nonreligious in many countries, with the larger increases coming in populations that had a higher standard of living. WIN/Gallup International, "Global Index of Religion and Atheism," August 6, 2012, http://www.wingia.com/en/news/win_gallup_international_ae_religiosity_and_atheism_index_ao_reveals_atheists_are_a_small_minority_in_the_early_years_of_21st_century/14/. In some countries that lack democratic institutions and reliable guarantees of free speech, polling is difficult, but, again, the precise numbers are less significant than the overall trend.

3. Barry Kosmin and Ariela Keysar, *American Religious Identification Survey Summary Report* (Hartford, CT: Institute for the Study of Secularism in Society & Culture, 2009), p. 8 (hereinafter "*ARIS*").

4. Pew Forum on Religion & Public Life, *Nones on the Rise: One-in-Five Adults Have No Religious Affiliation* (Washington, DC: Pew Research Center, 2012), pp. 9–10, http://www.pewforum.org/Unaffiliated/nones-on-the-rise.aspx.

5. Barry Kosmin and Ariela Keyser, *Religious, Spiritual, and Secular: The Emergence of Three Distinct Worldviews Among American College*

Students (Hartford, CT: Institute for the Study of Secularism in Society & Culture, 2013). The report is available at http://commons.trincoll.edu/aris/publications/2013-2/2013-2/.

6. Kosmin and Keysar, *ARIS*, p. 8.

7. For the view that religion may be on the rebound, see John Micklethwait and Adrian Wooldridge, *God Is Back: How the Global Revival of Faith Is Changing the World* (New York: Penguin Books, 2010).

8. For example, see his address in Scotland in September 2010, in which he alluded to totalitarian regimes as being the end result of aggressive secularism. NBCNews.com, "Pope Warns of 'Aggressive' Secularism in U.K.," September 16, 2010, http://www.nbcnews.com/id/39207225/.

9. Newt Gingrich, *To Save America: Stopping Obama's Secular-Socialist Machine* (Washington, DC: Regnery Publishing, 2010).

10. Michael Gerson, "What Atheists Can't Answer," *Washington Post*, July 13, 2007.

11. "Notes on Virginia," in *The Separation of Church and State: Writings on a Fundamental Freedom by America's Founders*, ed. Forrest Church (Boston: Beacon Press, 2004), pp. 51–52.

Chapter 2: The Birth of the Secular State

1. S. Harrison Thomson, *Europe in Renaissance and Reformation* (New York: Harcourt, Brace & World, 1963), p. 739.

2. Marvin R. O'Connell, *The Counter-Reformation 1559–1610* (New York: Harper & Row, 1974), p. 172.

3. See generally Francis Oakley, "Christian Obedience and Authority, 1520–1550," in *The Cambridge History of Political Thought 1450–1700*, ed. J. H. Burns (Cambridge: Cambridge University Press, 1991), pp. 159–192.

4. Aquinas, *Summa Theologica*, II–II, question 11, art. 3.

5. *Two Treatises of Government*, ed. Thomas L. Cook (1690; New York: Hafner Publishing Company, 1947), pp. 168–169, (bk. 2, chapter VIII).

6. *A Letter Concerning Toleration* (1689; Amherst, NY: Prometheus Books, 1990).

7. Ibid., p. 18.

8. Ibid., pp. 18, 19.

9. Ibid., p. 20.

10. Ibid., pp. 19–21. A good contemporary analysis of Locke's arguments is found in Russell Blackford, *Freedom of Religion & The Secular State* (Chichester, UK: Wiley-Blackwell, 2012), pp. 34–55.

11. *A Letter Concerning Toleration*, p. 64.

12. Ibid., p. 64.

13. Isaac Kramnick and R. Laurence Moore, *The Godless Constitution: A Moral Defense of the Secular State* (New York: W. W. Norton & Co., 2005), p. 72. See also Bernard Bailyn, *The Ideological Origins of the American Revolution* (Cambridge, MA: The Belknap Press, 1967), p. 27 ("In pamphlet after pamphlet the American writers cited Locke on natural rights and on the social and government contract").

14. Martha C. Nussbaum, *Liberty of Conscience: In Defense of America's Tradition of Religious Equality* (New York: Basic Books, 2008), pp. 38–39, 45–46; Nathaniel Philbrick, *Mayflower: A Story of Courage, Community, and War* (New York: Viking, 2006), p. 177.

15. Jonathan Elliot, *The Debates in the Several State Conventions on the Adoption of the Federal Constitution*, 2nd ed. (Philadelphia: J.B. Lippincott & Co., 1876), vol. 3, p. 330, http://memory.loc.gov/cgi-bin/query/r?ammem/hlaw:@field(DOCID+@lit(ed00313)).

16. Ibid., p. 657.

17. Adrienne Koch and William Peden, eds., *The Life and Selected Writings of Thomas Jefferson* (New York: Random House, 1944), pp. 462–464.

18. For a summary and analysis of the debate in Congress over the religion clauses of the First Amendment, see Douglas Laycock, "Nonpreferential Aid to Religion: A False Claim About Original Intent," *William and Mary Law Review* 27 (1986): 875–923; Leonard W. Levy, *The Establishment Clause: Religion and the First Amendment* (New York: Macmillan, 1986), esp. pp. 75–84.

19. Laycock, "Nonpreferential Aid to Religion," pp. 882–883.

20. David Barton, the founder of WallBuilders, a Christian Right organization that describes its mission as presenting "America's forgotten history and heroes," is the author most commonly associated with the Christian nation viewpoint, http://www.wallbuilders.com/ABTbioDB. asp. Barton is a prolific writer. Perhaps his best work is *Original Intent: The Courts, the Constitution, & Religion*, 2nd ed. (Aledo, TX: WallBuilder Press, 1997). Another Christian nation advocate is Cynthia Dunbar, *One Nation Under God: How the Left Is Trying To Erase What Made Us Great* (Oviedo, FL: HigherLife Development Services, 2008). An analysis and critique of the Christian nation position can be found in Kerry Walters, "The Myth of America's Christian Heritage," *Free Inquiry* 32 (June–July 2012): pp. 18–22.

21. The Fundamental Orders of 1639 can be found at the website of Yale Law School's Avalon Project, http://avalon.law.yale.edu/17th_century/order. asp.

22. This petition is reprinted in Forrest Church, ed., *The Separation of Church and State: Writings on a Fundamental Freedom by America's Founders* (Boston: Beacon Press, 2004), pp. 60–71.

23. The ruling is *Cantwell v. Connecticut*, 310 U.S. 296 (1940).

24. Alexis De Tocqueville, *Democracy in America*, trans. and ed. Harvey C. Mansfield and Delba Winthrop (Chicago: University of Chicago Press, 2010), p. 280.

25. See, for example, Sabrina Ramet, ed., *Religious Policy in the Soviet Union* (Cambridge: Cambridge University Press, 1993).

Chapter 3: From the Secular State to the Secular Society

1. Jacques Berlinerblau, *How To Be Secular: A Call to Arms for Religious Freedom* (New York: Houghton Mifflin Harcourt, 2012), p. 57.

2. Richard Rorty, "Religion as a Conversation-stopper," in *Philosophy and Social Hope* (London: Penguin Books, 1999), pp.168–174, 171. Rorty subsequently backpedaled a bit. See his essay "Religion in the Public Square: A Reconsideration," *Journal of Religious Ethics* 31 (2003): pp. 141–149. Rorty despaired of articulating a principled basis for completely excluding religion from public policy debates, although he still maintained that one should not be able to rely solely on religious doctrine in a policy debate. As is evident

from my argument, I believe Rorty conceded too much.

3. Ralph Reed, "Immigration Rights and Wrongs," *USA Today*, Feb. 12, 2013, http://www.usatoday.com/story/opinion/2013/02/12/ralph-reed-immigration-rights-and-wrongs/1914813/.

4. David K. Ryden, ed., *Is the Good Book Good Enough? Evangelical Perspectives on Public Policy* (Lanham, MD: Lexington Books, 2011) (hereinafter "*Good Book*").

5. David. K. Ryden, "Introduction," in *Good Book*, p. 9.

6. See the essay by David K. Ryden and Jeffrey J. Polet, "Love Rightly Understood: Reflections on the Substance, Style, and Spirit of Evangelical Activism and (Same-Sex) Marriage Policy," in *Good Book*, pp. 185–204, esp. pp. 194–201.

7. 403 U.S. 602 (1971).

8. *Epperson v. Arkansas*, 393 U.S. 97 (1968). For a thorough discussion of the secular purpose test, see Andrew Koppelman, "Secular Purpose," *Virginia Law Review* 88 (2002): 87–166.

9. See also Kent Greenawalt, *Religious Convictions and Public Choice* (New York: Oxford University Press, 1988).

10. John Rawls, *A Theory of Justice* (Cambridge, MA: The Belknap Press, 1971), p. 213.

11. Ibid.

12. Ibid.

13. John Rawls, *Political Liberalism* (New York: Columbia University Press, 1996), p. 224.

14. Bruce Ackerman, *Social Justice in the Liberal State* (New Haven, CT: Yale University Press, 1980), p. 10.

15. Ibid., p. 127.

16. Jeffrey Stout, *Democracy and Tradition* (Princeton, NJ: Princeton University Press, 2004); J. Caleb Clanton, *Religion and Democratic Citizenship: Inquiry and Conviction in the American Public Square* (Lanham, MD: Lexington Books, 2008) (hereinafter "*Religion and Democratic Citizenship*").

17. *Democracy and Tradition*, p. 69.

18. *Religion and Democratic Citizenship*, esp. pp. 108–144, 128–138.

19. For a discussion of the alternative gospels, see Elaine Pagels, *The Gnostic Gospels* (New York: Radom House, 1979). According to Pagels, with the alternative gospels coming to light, "We now begin to see that what we call Christianity—and what we identify as Christian tradition—actually represents only a small selection of specific sources, chosen from among dozens of others" (p. xxxviii). For a discussion of some of the difficulties in determining the historicity of Jesus, see R. Joseph Hoffmann, ed., *Sources of the Jesus Tradition: Separating History from Myth* (Amherst, NY: Prometheus Books, 2010).

20. Excerpt from Letter to Edward Newenham, 20 October 1792, in Albert J. Menendez and Edd Doerr, eds., *Great Quotations on Religious Freedom* (Amherst, NY: Prometheus Books, 2002), p. 126.

21. Adele M. Stan, "Catholic Bishops' Allies Dominate Hearing on Sweeping Anti-Choice Bill," *RH Reality Check*, January 9, 2014, http://rhrealitycheck.org/article/2014/01/09/catholic-bishops-allies-dominate-hearing-on-sweeping-anti-choice-bill/.

22. National Bioethics Advisory Commission, *Cloning Human Beings* (Rockville, MD: Government Printing Office, 1997), esp. pp. 39–61. See also Transcript of Testimony Before National Bioethics Advisory Commission, March 13 and 14, 1997. Available at bioethics.georgetown.edu/nbac/transcripts/1997/3-13-97.pdf and bioethics.georgetown.edu/nbac/transcripts/1997/3-14-97.pdf.

23. Stephen L. Carter, *The Culture of Disbelief: How American Law and Politics Trivialize Religious Devotion* (New York: Anchor Books, 1994) (hereinafter "*Culture of Disbelief*"), p. 216.

24. Noah Feldman, *Divided by God* (New York: Farrar, Straus and Giroux, 2005), p. 224.

25. Carter, *Culture of Disbelief*, pp. 55–56.

26. See, for example, the website "Islam Question and Answer," http://islamqa.info/en/.

27. *An Essay Concerning Human Understanding*, bk. IV, chap. 19, sec. 5.

28. Ibid., sec. 14.

29. Carter, *Culture of Disbelief*, p. 226.

30. Ibid., p. 232.

31. Ibid., p. 291 n. 11.

32. Ibid., p. 227.

33. Indeed, it was not until 1995 that the Southern Baptist Convention apologized for its opposition to both the antislavery and civil rights movements. Southern Baptist Convention, "Resolution on Racial Reconciliation on the 150th Anniversary of the Southern Baptist Convention" (June 1995), http://www.sbc.net/resolutions/amResolution.asp?ID=899.

34. Martin Luther, *On the Jews and Their Lies*, trans. Martin H. Bertram, vol. 47 of *Luther's Works* (Philadelphia: Fortress Press, 1971).

Chapter 4: Why God Can't Tell Us What to Do

1. Pew Research Center, "Pew Global Attitudes Project" (Washington, DC: Pew Research Center, 2007), p. 33. Available at http://www.pewglobal.org/files/pdf/258.pdf.

2. Ibid.

3. See, for example, Hemant Mehta, "What Percentage of Prisoners Are Atheists? It's a Lot Smaller Than We Ever Imagined," *Friendly Atheist*, July 16, 2013. Available at: http://www.patheos.com/blogs/friendlyatheist/2013/07/16/what-percentage-of-prisoners-are-atheists-its-a-lot-smaller-than-we-ever-imagined/ (discussing religious self-identification survey of prisoners in federal system; percentage of self-identified atheist prisoners less than 0.1%). See also Pew Research Center, *Religion in Prisons: A 50-State Survey of Prison Chaplains* (Washington, D.C.: Pew Research Center, 2012), p. 48. Available at: http://www.pewforum.org/Social-Welfare/prison-chaplains-preface.aspx (interviews with prison chaplains indicate about 10.6 percent of prison population has no religious preference; unclear how "no religious preference" correlates with atheism and agnosticism).

4. Philip Kitcher, in his magisterial work, *The Ethical Project* (Cambridge, MA: Harvard University Press, 2011), also takes a functionalist approach to morality. He describes the functions of morality in different terms—for him,

morality promotes social harmony by remedying failures of altruism—but his approach is broadly consistent with mine.

5. *Leviathan*, chap. 13.9.

6. Kitcher, in *The Ethical Project*, provides a persuasive description of the development of moral norms within small human communities and their eventual extension to larger human communities. See esp. pp. 67–110. See also Peter Singer, *The Expanding Circle: Ethics, Evolution, and Moral Progress* (New York: Farrar, Straus & Giroux, 1981).

7. *Culture of Disbelief*, p. 226.

8. See Transcript of Oral Argument in *Van Orden v. Perry*, Case No. 03–1500, p. 29. Available at http://www.supremecourtus.gov/oral_arguments/argument_transcripts/03-1500.pdf. *Van Orden v. Perry*, 545 U.S. 677 (2005) was a challenge to the placement of a Ten Commandments monument on the grounds of the Texas state capitol. In his remarks at oral argument, Justice Scalia indicated he regarded God as the authoritative source of law and morality.

9. *Euthyphro*, esp. 6d–10e.

10. *Summa Theologica*, I-II, question 94, art. 5.

11. The Church of Jesus Christ of Latter-day Saints, "Excerpts from Three Addresses by President Wilford Woodruff Regarding the Manifesto," http://www.lds.org/scriptures/dc-testament/od/1?lang=eng.

12. "The Transmission of Divine Revelation," *Catechism of the Catholic Church*, Part 1, sec.1, chap. 2, art. 2. Available at http://www.vatican.va/archive/ccc_css/archive/catechism/p1s1c2a2.htm#80.

13. "Dogmatic Constitution on Divine Revelation," chap. 1, sec. 6 (promulgated Nov. 18, 1965) http://www.vatican.va/archive/hist_councils/ii_vatican_council/documents/vat-ii_const_19651118_dei-verbum_en.html.

14. *Leviathan*, chap. 32.6.

15. Ingrid Mattson, *The Story of the Qur'an: Its History and Place in Muslim Life* (Oxford: Blackwell Publishing, 2008), pp. 17–18.

16. *City of God*, 19.9.

17. For appearances by pagan deities, see Robin Lane Fox, *Pagans and*

Christians (New York: Alfred A. Knopf, 1987), pp. 102–167.

18. "Dogmatic Constitution on Divine Revelation," chap. 1, sec. 5.

19. *Crossing the Threshold of Hope* (New York: Alfred A. Knopf, 1994), p. 10.

20. The Abbas speech is quoted in an essay by David Makovsky and Ghaith Al-Omari, "Talking Up a Two-State Solution," *Washington Post*, March 1, 2013.

21. *Euthyphro*, 8b. I am using the translation of Lane Cooper found in Edith Hamilton and Huntington Cairns, eds., *Plato: The Collected Dialogues* (Princeton, NJ: Princeton University Press, 1961).

22. T. M. Luhrmann, *When God Talks Back: Understanding the American Evangelical Relationship with God* (New York: Vintage Books, 2012).

Chapter 5: The Common Morality and the Objectivity That Matters

1. *Hamlet*, act 2, scene 2, lines 253–254.

2. *A Treatise of Human Nature*, ed. L. A. Selby-Bigge (Oxford: Oxford University Press, 1888), p. 469.

3. *Enquiries Concerning Human Understanding and Concerning the Principles of Morals*, ed. L. A. Selby-Bigge, 3rd rev. ed. P. H. Nidditch (Oxford: Oxford University Press, 1975), pp. 272–273 (hereinafter "*Enquiries*").

4. Sissela Bok, *Common Values* (Columbia, MO: University of Missouri Press, 1995), p. 15.

5. The most interesting live issue regarding the scope of morality is not whether we should exclude some humans from the scope of morality but whether we should include nonhuman animals within the moral community. See, for example, Peter Singer, *In Defense of Animals: The Second Wave* (Oxford: Blackwell, 2006). My own view is that although we have some obligations toward animals, for example, the obligation to refrain from cruelty, we are not obliged to give equal consideration to the interests of nonhuman animals. Ronald A. Lindsay, *Future Bioethics: Overcoming Taboos, Myths, and Dogmas* (Amherst, NY: Prometheus Books, 2008), pp. 261–274.

6. How evolution shaped our dispositions so that we became capable of

altruistic conduct and responsive to moral norms is a complex, fascinating subject in itself. It's also a topic that has generated much controversy. The best summary of how evolution has created dispositions to moral conduct is found in *Ethical Project*, esp. pp. 17–137. One of the major disputes regarding the role of evolution is whether we need to posit group evolution to explain the development of morality. Compare Edward O. Wilson, *The Social Conquest of Earth* (New York: Liveright Publishing Corporation, 2012) with Richard Dawkins, "The Descent of Edward Wilson," *Prospect*, May 24, 2012, http://www.prospectmagazine.co.uk/magazine/edward-wilson-social-conquest-earth-evolutionary-errors-origin-species/. I am skeptical of group evolution, but I am not going to explore this controversy here because, although this is an important issue, it is tangential to the focus of my discussion. How we evolved moral dispositions may be disputed, but few seriously dispute that we have such dispositions.

7. Aristotle, *Nicomachean Ethics*, 10.9 1179b15–30.

8. *Enquiries*, pp. 170, 271.

9. Jonathan Haidt, *The Righteous Mind: Why Good People Are Divided by Politics and Religion* (New York: Pantheon Books, 2012) (hereinafter "*The Righteous Mind*"), p. 268.

10. BBC News, "Priests Brawl in Bethlehem's Church of the Nativity," Dec. 28, 2011, http://www.bbc.co.uk/news/world-middle-east-16347418.

11. Steven Pinker, *The Better Angels of Our Nature: How Violence Has Declined* (New York: Viking Penguin, 2011); Lawrence H. Keeley, *War Before Civilization* (New York: Oxford University Press, 1996).

12. Hugh Thomas, *The Slave Trade* (New York: Simon & Schuster, 1997) (hereinafter "*Slave Trade*"); David B. Davis, *The Problem of Slavery in Western Culture* (Ithaca, NY: Cornell University Press, 1966) (hereinafter "*Problem of Slavery*").

13. *Problem of Slavery*, p. 47. In some cultures, a member of the community could lose his moral status through committing a crime or failing to repay a debt, in which case he too could become a slave.

14. Ibid., p. 100.

15. *Slave Trade*, p. 65.

16. Ibid., esp. pp. 467–485.

17. Universal Declaration of Human Rights, http://www.un.org/en/documents/udhr/index.shtml.

18. One of the most comprehensive, biblically based set of arguments in favor of slavery is found in Josiah Priest, *Bible Defence of Slavery: And Origin, Fortunes and History of the Negro Race* (Glasgow, KY: W.S. Brown, 1852), http://books.google.com/books?id=ilcSAAAAIAAJ&printsec=frontcover&source=gbs_ge_summary_r&cad=0#v=onepage&q&f=false. Priest was a Christian cleric.

19. Convention of Ministers, *An Address to Christians Throughout the World* (1863), https://archive.org/details/addresstochristi01slsn.

20. Aileen S. Kraditor, *The Ideas of the Woman Suffrage Movement, 1890–1920* (New York: W. W. Norton & Company, 1981), pp. 75–76 (hereinafter "*Ideas of Woman Suffrage Movement*").

21. *Bradwell v. State*, 83 U.S. 130, 141 (1872).

22. For a discussion of some of the outrages against women that have been justified by appeals to religion, see Ophelia Benson and Jeremy Stangroom, *Does God Hate Women?* (New York: Continuum Books, 2009).

23. *Ideas of Woman Suffrage Movement*, pp. 43–55.

24. Ibid., pp. 75–82.

25. John Stuart Mill, "On the Subjection of Women," in *On Liberty and Other Essays*, ed. John Gray (Oxford: Oxford University Press, 1998), pp. 471–582.

26. Susan Jacoby, *The Great Agnostic: Robert Ingersoll and American Freethought* (New Haven, CT: Yale University Press, 2013), pp. 117–125.

27. Eleanor Flexner and Ellen Fitzpatrick, *Century of Struggle: The Woman's Rights Movement in the United States* (Cambridge, MA: The Belknap Press, 1975), p. 280.

28. Matthew O'Brien, "God and Moral Absolutes," December 13, 2011, http://www.thepublicdiscourse.com/2011/12/4433/. For a more detailed, scholarly defense of absolute moral norms and their connection to religion, see John Finnis, *Moral Absolutes: Tradition, Revision, and Truth* (Washington, D.C.: Catholic University of America Press, 1991).

29. W. D. Ross, *The Right and the Good* (Oxford: Clarendon Press, 1930), esp. pp. 19–36.

30. John Paul II, *The Gospel of Life* (New York: Random House, 1995), p. 102.

31. This distinction between intending to stop treatment and intending to bring about the patient's death was endorsed by the Supreme Court in *Vacco v. Quill*, 521 U.S. 793 (1997).

Chapter 6: Morality Without a Supernatural Net

1. This is an excerpt from the play *Sisyphus*. We no longer have the complete play. This excerpt was quoted by Sextus Empiricus and can be found in Sextus Empiricus, *Against Physicists. Against Ethicists*, trans. Robert G. Bury, vol. III in Loeb Classical Library edition of works of Sextus Empiricus (Cambridge, MA: Harvard University Press, 1997), p. 31. As the excerpt is not only from a play but a play that is no longer extant, caution must be utilized in attributing the sentiments in the poem to Critias. To complicate matters further, there is a scholarly debate over whether *Sisyphus* is a work by Critias or Euripides. See Jan N. Bremmer, "Atheism in Antiquity," in *The Cambridge Companion to Atheism*, ed. Michael Martin (New York: Cambridge University Press, 2007), pp. 11–26, esp. pp. 16–18. But whoever the author and whether or not the excerpt represents the view of the author or merely a character in the play, the excerpt indicates that some skeptics thought belief in God served an instrumental purpose.

2. "Boy Scouts of America Kick Out 19 Year Old Eagle Scout for Being Atheist," Scouting for All press release, October 26, 2002, http://www.scoutingforall.org/data/archives/aaic/2002102901.html.

3. Jeffrey M. Jones, "Atheists, Muslims See Most Bias as Presidential Candidates," *Gallup*, June 21, 2012, http://www.gallup.com/poll/155285/atheists-muslims-bias-presidential-candidates.aspx.

4. Penny Edgell, Joseph Gerteis, and Douglas Hartmann, "Atheists as 'Other': Moral Boundaries and Cultural Membership in American Society," *American Sociological Review* 71 (2006): pp. 211–234, 218.

5. Ibid., p. 227.

6. Ibid., p. 228

7. Ibid., p. 230.

8. Ronald E. Smith, Gregory Wheeler, and Edward Diener, "Faith Without Works: Jesus People, Resistance to Temptation, and Altruism," *Journal of Applied Social Psychology* 5 (1975): pp. 320–330.

9. Azim F. Shariff and Ara Norenzayan, "Mean Gods Make Good People: Different Views of God Predict Cheating Behavior," *International Journal for the Psychology of Religion* 21 (2011): p. 85–96 (hereinafter "*Mean Gods*"); Clifford Nowell and Doug Laufer, "Undergraduate Cheating in the Fields of Business and Economics," *The Journal of Economic Education* 28 (1997): pp. 3–12. Consistent with several other previous studies, the *Mean Gods* study found that there is no correlation between cheating and belief in God. However, it suggests there may be a correlation between believing in a wrathful, punishing God and lower cheating rates. Further study of this connection should be conducted. Perhaps the New Testament will have to be discarded in favor of the Old Testament.

10. Psychopaths account for between 15 and 35 percent of the United States prison population. Kent A. Kiehl and Joshua W. Buckholtz, "Inside the Mind of a Psychopath," *Scientific American Mind*, September–October 2010, pp. 22–29.

11. Adolf Hitler, *Mein Kampf*, trans. Helmut Ripperger (New York: Reynal & Hitchcock, 1940), see, for example, pp. 289, 392, 422–423.

12. Ibid., pp. 365, 574.

13. See, for example, Norman H. Baynes, ed., *The Speeches of Adolf Hitler April 1922–August 1939* (Oxford: Oxford University Press, 1942), vol. 1, pp. 333–412.

14. Ibid., pp. 386–387.

15. An accessible survey article on the academic literature addressing the supposed "prosocial" effects of religion is Luke W. Galen and Jeremy Beahan, "A Skeptical Review of Religious Prosociality Research," *Free Inquiry* 33, no. 4 (2013): pp. 14–22.

16. A summary of some of the research and the different methodologies employed may be found in Chang-Ho C. Ji, Lori Pendergraft, and Matthew Perry, "Religiosity, Altruism, and Altruistic Hypocrisy: Evidence from Protestant Adolescents," *Review of Religious Research* 48 (2006): pp. 156–178.

17. Robert D. Putnam and David E. Campbell, *American Grace: How Religion Divides and Unites Us* (New York: Simon & Schuster, 2010) (hereinafter *"American Grace"*).

18. Ibid., p. 444.

19. Ibid., p. 473.

20. On this point, see *The Righteous Mind*, pp. 52–61.

21. For a discussion of priming, see Jonah Berger and Grainne Fitzsimmons, "Dogs on the Street, Pumas on Your Feet: How Cues in the Environment Influence Product Evaluation and Choice," *Journal of Marketing Research* 45 (2008): pp. 1–14. The connection between cue and mental representation may be very indirect. Seeing dogs may incline one to prefer Puma brand sneakers, even though a Puma is not a dog.

22. Deepak Malhotra, "(When) Are Religious People Nicer? Religious Salience and the 'Sunday Effect' on Pro-Social Behavior," *Judgment and Decision-Making* 5, no. 2 (2010): pp. 138–143.

23. *American Grace*, pp. 454–458.

24. Ibid., p. 454.

25. Eleanor Goldberg, "Library Rejects $3,000 Donation from Atheist Blogger, Saying He Belongs to 'Hate Group'," *Huffington Post*, December 20, 2013, http://www.huffingtonpost.com/2013/12/20/library-rejects-atheist-donation_n_4481422.html?ir=Books&ref=topbar.

26. *Society Without God*, p. 28.

27. Ibid., pp. 74–75.

28. *American Grace*, p. 483.

29. The Pew Forum on Religion & Public Life, *Can Civilization Survive Without God?: A Conversation with Christopher and Peter Hitchens*, October 12, 2010, http://www.pewforum.org/Belief-in-God/Can-Civilization-Survive-Without-God-.aspx.

30. Jonathan Sacks, *The Great Partnership: Science, Religion, and the Search for Meaning* (New York: Schocken Books, 2011).

31. Ibid., p. 144.

32. Ibid., pp. 146–147.

33. Ibid., p. 150.

34. Ibid., p. 152.

35. For a good discussion of attitudes among the ancient Greeks regarding suicide and euthanasia, see John M. Cooper, "Greek Philosophers on Euthanasia and Suicide," in *Suicide and Euthanasia: Historical and Contemporary Themes*, ed. Baruch A. Brody (Dordrecht: Kluwer, 1989), pp. 9–38.

36. For an analysis of the modern decline in homicide rates, and of violence in general, see Steven Pinker, *The Better Angels of Our Nature: Why Violence Has Declined* (New York: Viking Penguin, 2011).

37. Phil Zuckerman, "Atheism, Secularity, and Well-Being: How the Findings of Social Science Counter Negative Stereotypes and Assumptions," *Sociology Compass* 3 (2009): pp. 949–971, p. 955.

Chapter 7: Secular Moral Reasoning and Public Policy

1. Michael Lipka, "5 Facts About Americans' Views on Life and Death Issues" (Washington, DC: Pew Research Center), January 7, 2014, http://www.pewresearch.org/fact-tank/2014/01/07/5-facts-about-americans-views-on-life-and-death-issues/.

2. Linda Ganzini et al., "Physicians' Experiences with the Oregon Death with Dignity Act," *New England Journal of Medicine* 342 (2000): 557–563 (hereinafter "Physicians' Experiences").

3. Oregon Division of Public Health, *Fifteenth Annual Report on Death with Dignity Act* (2013), p. 1. This report is available at http://public.health.oregon.gov/ProviderPartnerResources/EvaluationResearch/DeathwithDignityAct/Pages/ar-index.aspx.

4. Oregon Division of Public Health, *Death with Dignity Act Requirements* (2006). This report is available at http://public.health.oregon.gov/ProviderPartnerResources/EvaluationResearch/DeathwithDignityAct/Pages/ar-index.aspx. See also Ronald A. Lindsay, "Oregon's Experience: Evaluating the Record," *American Journal of Bioethics* 9 (2009): 19–27, 23.

5. See Kathleen Foley and Herbert Hendin, "The Oregon Experiment," in *The Case Against Assisted Suicide: For the Right to End-of-Life Care*, ed. K. Foley and H. Hendin (Baltimore, MD: The Johns Hopkins University Press, 2002), pp.144–174 (hereinafter "The Oregon Experiment"); New York State Task Force on Life and the Law, *When Death Is Sought: Assisted Suicide and Euthanasia in the Medical Context* (New York: New York State Task Force on Life and the Law, 1994), esp. pp. 93–96, 99–103.

6. "Physicians' Experiences," 557–563.

7. Oregon Division of Public Health, *Fifteenth Annual Report on Death with Dignity Act* (2013), p. 4.

8. For a discussion of the moral significance of disparate impact in the context of assisted dying, see Ronald A. Lindsay, "Should We Impose Quotas? Evaluating the 'Disparate Impact' Argument Against Legalization of Assisted Suicide," *Journal of Law, Medicine, & Ethics* 30 (2002): 6–16.

9. Oregon Division of Public Health, *Fifteenth Annual Report on Death with Dignity Act* (2013), p. 4; Washington State Department of Health, *Death with Dignity Act Report* (2012), p. 1. This report is available at http://www.doh.wa.gov/YouandYourFamily/IllnessandDisease/DeathwithDignityAct.aspx.

10. Bonnie Steinbock, "The Case for Physician Assisted Suicide: Not (Yet) Proven," *Journal of Medical Ethics* 31 (2005): 235–241.

11. Oregon Division of Public Health, *Fifteenth Annual Report on Death with Dignity Act* (2013), pp. 4–5.

12. For contrasting perspectives on the few alleged cases of abuse in Oregon, compare "The Oregon Experiment," pp. 144–174 with Peter Goodwin, "The Distortion of Cases in Oregon," in *Physician-Assisted Dying: The Case for Palliative Care & Patient Choice*, ed. T. Quill and M. Battin, (Baltimore, MD: The Johns Hopkins University Press, 2004), pp.184–189.

13. For a secular argument for the position that intentionally taking another's life is always wrong, see Neil M. Gorsuch, *The Future of Assisted Suicide and Euthanasia* (Princeton, NJ: Princeton University Press, 2006), esp. pp. 157–166.

14. In *Vacco v. Quill*, 521 U.S. 793 (1997), the U.S. Supreme Court attempted to distinguish between withdrawal of treatment and assistance in

dying, in part, on the ground that the former is merely allowing the patient to die from the underlying disease.

15. This is the distinction on which Gorsuch (see note 13) relies heavily. For an extended critique of the use of "intention" to distinguish between cases involving withdrawal of treatment from cases involving assisted dying, see *Future Bioethics*, pp. 82–83.

Chapter 8: Living Together

1. Harvey Cox, *The Secular City: Secularization and Urbanization in Theological Perspective* 25th anniversary ed., (New York: Collier Books, 1990), p. 31. The age of Cox's book (first published in 1965) is revealed by the use of his term "man" for "humanity." Cox's work remains relevant despite its age. Cox was wrong about the decline of fundamentalist religion (he didn't foresee either the rise of the Christian Right in the United States or the rise of Islamic extremism in other parts of the world), but his general point that religion can survive in a secular society retains validity.

2. See Kitcher, *The Ethical Project*, esp. pp. 111–115. The term "unseen enforcer" is his.

3. Gary Langer, "Poll Finds Vast Gaps in Basic Views on Gender, Race, Religion and Politics," ABC News, October 28, 2013, http://abcnews.go.com/blogs/politics/2013/10/poll1-finds-vast-gaps-in-basic-views-on-gender-race-religion-and-politics/.

4. The RFRA is codified at 42 U.S.C. §2000bb-1. The RLUIPA is codified at 42 U.S.C. §2000cc.

5. Perhaps the best single work on this issue is Brian Leiter, *Why Tolerate Religion?* (Princeton, NJ: Princeton University Press, 2013). Blackford has a good analysis of religious exemptions in *Freedom of Religion & The Secular State*, pp. 94–117. In my own *Future Bioethics*, pp. 131–152, I discuss religious exemptions in the healthcare context.

6. 398 U. S. 333 (1970).

7. Ibid., p. 344.

8. Ibid., pp. 356–358.

9. Steve Paulson, "The Atheist Delusion," *Salon.com*, December 18,

2007, http://www.salon.com/2007/12/19/john_haught/. It is interesting that when someone like Richard Dawkins states that the beliefs of Young Earth creationists are ridiculous, he's censured for his lack of diplomacy, but asserting that atheists are either nihilists or inexcusably ignorant of the fact that they are committed to nihilism doesn't seem to inspire much criticism.

10. Bertrand Russell, "What I Believe," in *Why I Am Not A Christian* (New York: Simon and Schuster, 1957), p. 54.

INDEX

213

ABOUT THE AUTHOR

Ronald A. Lindsay is president and CEO of the Center for Inquiry and of its affiliates, the Council for Secular Humanism and the Committee for Skeptical Inquiry. He has a PhD in philosophy from Georgetown University, with a concentration in bioethics, and a JD from the University of Virginia. He is the author of the essay on "Euthanasia" in the *International Encyclopedia of Ethics* and of the book *Future Bioethics: Overcoming Taboos, Myths, and Dogmas.*